THE
BABE

A Life in Pictures

THE
BABE

A Life in Pictures

Lawrence S. Ritter

TEXT AND CAPTIONS

Mark Rucker

PICTURE EDITOR

A BASEBALL INK BOOK

TICKNOR & FIELDS · NEW YORK · 1988

For Rolf Preuss,
a true friend,
a wonderful person
                L.S.R.

For my family
                M.R.

For information about permission to reproduce selections
from this book, write to Permissions, Ticknor & Fields,
52 Vanderbilt Avenue, New York, New York 10017.

LIBRARY OF CONGRESS CATALOGING-IN-PUBLICATION DATA

Ritter, Lawrence S.
    The Babe: a life in pictures / text by Lawrence S. Ritter;
picture research by Mark Rucker.
        p.   cm.   (A Baseball Ink book)
    Bibliography: p.
    Includes index.
    ISBN 0-89919-768-X
    1. Ruth, Babe, 1895–1948. 2. Baseball players—United States—
Biography. I. Rucker, Mark. II. Title. III. Series.
GV865.R8R58 1988
796.357′092′4—dc19   88-8579
[B]   CIP

PRINTED IN THE UNITED STATES OF AMERICA

J 10 9 8 7 6 5 4 3 2 1

BOOK DESIGN BY SYLVIA FREZZOLINI

CONTENTS

Babe Ruth is, without a doubt, the greatest baseball player of all time.

That Babe Ruth is all-time number one is not obvious, of course, to millions of baseball fans who have grown up since World War II. To many of them, the name "Babe Ruth" sounds like ancient history, which is understandable in that he played his last major league game in 1935 and drew his last breath in 1948. His most famous records have been broken, and his luster as America's most idolized sports hero has inevitably been dimmed by the sheer passage of time.

The word "arguably" has come into fashionable usage in recent years. It is employed almost automatically in discussing comparative rankings—for example, "Reggie Jackson was arguably the most exciting ballplayer of the seventies." Well, fashionable or not, there is simply no place for "arguably" in connection with Babe Ruth's place in baseball history: the Babe was absolutely and unequivocally the greatest baseball player who ever lived. The purpose of this volume is to rescue Babe Ruth from the dusty files of history and, in words and pictures, to let those who were not alive in the twenties and thirties share the pleasure and excitement that Babe Ruth generated during his lifetime.

Those who were fortunate enough to have seen him can relive the experience through these pages and in their mind's eye. On a baseball field he was, for almost twenty years, the center of attention no matter what he was doing: from the time he first stepped out of the dugout for batting or fielding practice, hours before a game was scheduled to begin, until the last out in the ninth inning, most of the audience seemed mesmerized by his presence. Fans in the box seats and bleachers alike, at home or away, spent most of their time watching his every move.

"Look how he steps over the foul line every time he crosses it. See, he never steps right on it."

"Look, he's signing an autograph for somebody over in those box seats behind third base. See how he writes with his right hand even though he bats and throws lefty."

"Let's not leave yet. I know the Yankees are way behind, but if they can get two men on in the ninth he'll come up to bat again."

Nobody had to say who "he" was. Everybody understood.

They were waiting for "him" to "hit one." And a surprising percentage of the time, he did just that.

Ruth typically batted third in the Yankee batting order, followed by Lou Gehrig. As a result Gehrig, one of the game's greatest players, rarely received much attention. "When Ruth's time at bat is over and it's my turn," Gehrig remarked once, "the fans are still buzzing about what the Babe did, regardless of whether he belted a home run or struck out. They wouldn't notice it if I walked up to home plate on my hands, stood on my head, and held the bat between my toes."

Ruth's most celebrated records involved home runs: 60 in one season (1927) and 714 lifetime. His single-season record was broken after thirty-four years by Roger Maris, who hit 61 in 1961, and his lifetime mark was eventually exceeded by Hank Aaron, who ended his illustrious career in 1976 with 755.

Even so, it is still Babe Ruth, more than Roger Maris, Hank Aaron, or anyone else for that matter, who is identified most closely with the home run.

Maris hit 61 in 1961 despite unbearable pressure, but in no other year did he reach 40 and in only two other years did he hit as many as 30. It is ironic that the man who broke Ruth's single-season home run record was not primarily a home run hitter at all. He hit 275 home runs over a twelve-year career, on average a home run for every 18.5 times he came to bat.

The home run belongs to Ruth. He hit more than 50 four times, more than 40 eleven times, on average one every 11.8 times at bat. (Next comes Ralph Kiner, with a home run every 14.1 times at bat, followed by Harmon Killebrew, one every 14.2 times.)

Hank Aaron averaged a home run every 16.4 times at bat. He never hit as many as 50 in a single year. With all due credit to Aaron, he hit 41 more lifetime home runs than Ruth, but over his long career he came to bat almost 4,000 more times. At the pace Ruth hit homers, 4,000 more times

at bat would have meant another 340 round-trippers, for a total of 1,054!

Babe Ruth is the greatest baseball player of all time not only because he was the game's premier home run hitter. Before he hit home runs for a living, he was a pitcher. There is a widespread impression that he was a good pitcher but nothing extra-special. In fact, he was no less than the best left-handed pitcher of his era in the major leagues.

He led the American League in earned run average in 1916 (with an ERA of 1.75). That was no fluke: over the five-year period from 1915 to 1919 his ERA was a sparkling 2.16. He set a pitching record for consecutive scoreless World Series innings that lasted for forty-three years, until it was broken by Whitey Ford in 1961, the same year Roger Maris broke his home run record. In 1918 he had an earned run average of 2.22 and simultaneously batted .300 and tied for the home run crown.

He left the pitching mound not because he was a poor pitcher but because pitchers play only one day in four or five. Management and his teammates wanted his bat in the lineup every day.

Great as they were, Ruth's batting and pitching feats alone can hardly explain his virtual deification by the American public. His charismatic personality played a crucial role as well. Not that everybody loved the Babe. In fact, a lot of people didn't even like him, especially in his early years with the Boston Red Sox. Teammates Tris Speaker and Smoky Joe Wood thought he was a self-centered slob, and many others thought he was an uncouth ignoramus at best.

His image didn't improve a whole lot during the late teens and early twenties, when he made a habit of hitting umpires, going into the stands after heckling fans, and boozing all night long. In 1922 American League President Ban Johnson called his conduct "reprehensible . . . shocking to every American mother who permits her boy to go to a game."

But after each escapade Ruth apologized, promised he'd never do it again, and begged for forgiveness.

And always there were the home runs, the long booming record-setting drives that awed the players as much as the fans. They were so magnificent, and came in such profusion, that they went a long way toward excusing conduct that might otherwise have been considered unforgivable.

His character was multifaceted. In part the Babe was a thoughtless roughneck and in part he was kind, generous, and considerate of the feelings of others. In many ways he was irresponsible and yet at the same time he could be conscious of his obligations to his team, to the general public, and especially to younger fans.

He was a simple man, in the best sense of the word, straightforward and unpretentious, and his love for children was genuine. He also loved to drink—mostly beer, but bourbon or scotch would do in a pinch—and he was always hungry for food and women, though he was not a connoisseur of either. He was a glutton, not a gourmet.

His behavior was condemned but then condoned. "Why, he's just a big kid," they'd say, and smile indulgently.

All this contributed in some mysterious way to his appeal. Kids knew only that he was a one-of-a-kind home run hitter, but many adults apparently lived vicariously through his uninhibited larger-than-life exploits off the field as well as on.

With the passage of time, he slowly changed. He learned something about self-discipline, became more responsible, began to take the role of being an American icon more seriously. He had always been gregarious, friendly to a fault, and now the gentle side of his nature began to dominate. The young hellion gradually mellowed into a sociable teddy bear who enjoyed a game of bridge, a laugh, a drink, but most of all the companionship of old friends.

With few exceptions, ballplayers who played with or against Babe Ruth usually react the same way when his name is mentioned. They lean back, look away, and invariably smile, a smile of warmth, fondness, and pride.

Take Jimmy Austin, who played third base or was third base coach with the St. Louis Browns during all of Ruth's career: "The Babe! He was different. The Babe always had a twinkle in his eye and when he'd hit a homer against us he'd never trot past third without giving me a wink."

Or Goose Goslin, who played against Ruth for over a decade: "Babe Ruth was my hero. He was my idol. He was a picture up there at the plate. What a ballplayer. And such a sweet guy, too. I tried to copy everything he did, both on and off the field."

Rube Bressler played in the majors over the same time span as Ruth: "There was only one Babe Ruth. He went on the ball field like he was playing in a cow pasture, with cows for an audience. He never knew what fear or nervousness was. He played by instinct, sheer instinct. One of the greatest pitchers of all time and he could hit the ball twice as far as any other human being. He was a damn animal. They know when it's going to rain, things like that. Nature, that was Ruth!"

Both teammates and opponents of Ruth vividly remember the times when they played with or against him. To be able to say that they played in a game with Babe Ruth gives them a special pride and satisfaction. In their old age, it is apparent that they believe just having been on the same field with him validates their own careers, indeed to some extent their own lives. And that, after all is said and done, is the ultimate testimony to his greatness.

LAWRENCE S. RITTER

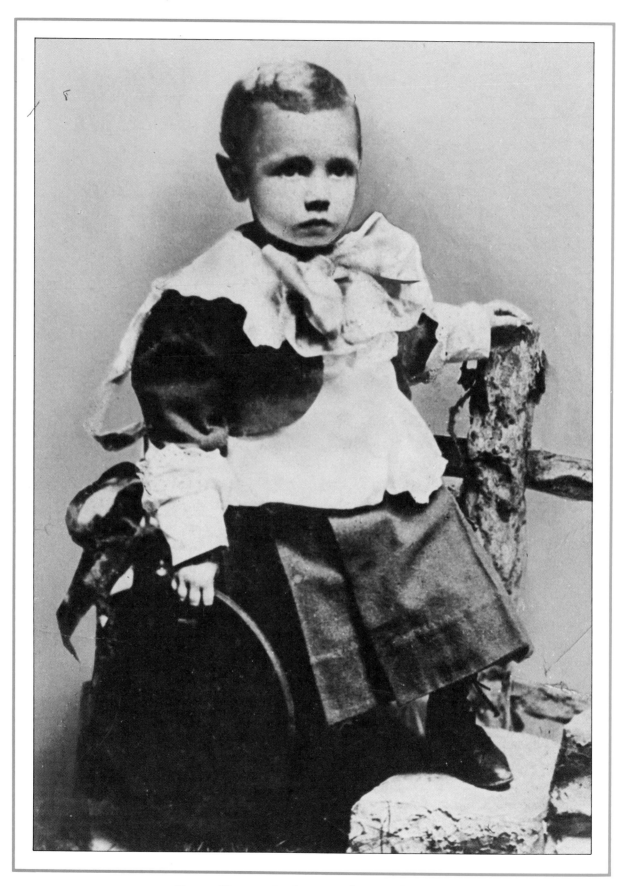

George Herman Ruth, Jr., at the age of three.

St. Mary's Industrial School for Boys

1895-1914

George Herman Ruth, Jr., was born on February 6, 1895, in his grandparents' house at 216 Emory Street in the tough, seedy waterfront section of Baltimore.

He died at 8:01 P.M. on August 16, 1948, in Memorial Hospital (now Memorial Sloan-Kettering) at 444 East Sixty-eighth Street in New York City.

For most of the intervening fifty-three and a half years, his life was an astonishing roller-coaster jamboree of mythic proportions: the undisciplined Ruthian express plunged boisterously down steep slopes and careened recklessly around unmarked curves—accompanied by a ceaseless shower of applause and adulation. In his heyday, as the following pages attest, he was the most frequently photographed person in the nation. As a result, by the late 1920s the former Baltimore waterfront urchin had become the best-known—and most idolized—person in the entire country.

How this wildly improbable metamorphosis came to pass, this implausible transformation from juvenile delinquent to virtual deity, is the subject matter of this book.

Kate Ruth (née Schamberger) was nineteen and George Herman Ruth twenty-three when their first child, George, Jr., was born in February of 1895. The young father earned his living as a bartender in a combination grocery store and saloon near the Baltimore waterfront.

Subsequently the Ruths had seven more children, but six died in infancy and only one (Mary Margaret, who came to be called Mamie, born in 1900) survived to adulthood. Soon after Mamie's birth her father opened his own tavern, at 426 West Camden Street, and the family moved into an apartment upstairs above the bar.

Kate's health was never robust, and she tried to spend as much time as possible helping her husband in the saloon, which was open long hours into the night. She had no time or patience for little George, who learned to crawl and walk on sawdust-covered saloon floors and was soon roaming through the rough waterfront district more or less on his own.

The youngster never had a real childhood in the usual sense of the word. His earliest memories were of street fights, stealing from shopkeepers, throwing rocks at deliverymen, and fleeing from cops through narrow cobblestoned alleys. He rarely went to school and for all practical purposes survived on the streets without direction or supervision.

"I think my mother hated me," he told a friend many years later, and he hardly ever mentioned his father during all of his adult life.

In mid-1902 Kate and her husband finally decided they no longer wanted the boy. On June 13, 1902, the father took his son by trolley car to St. Mary's Industrial School for Boys and—despite the child's tears and protestations—signed him over to the custody of a group of men dressed ominously in full-length black gowns. It must have been a terrifying experience for a seven-year-old.

Although the youngster could hardly realize it then, this was to be his home for a long, long time. On a few occasions he was "paroled" to live with his family, but sooner or later his parents always brought him back. He would not leave St. Mary's for good until February 27, 1914, as a fully grown nineteen-year-old young man.

The institution that accepted custody of the youth consisted of six multistory gray stone buildings huddled together four miles southwest of downtown Baltimore. The buildings occupied several acres surrounded by a wall that imparted a distinct prison atmosphere, especially since guards were always on duty. The guards were there because St. Mary's was a combination reformatory (or "reform school," as such institutions were popularly called then) and orphanage, with emphasis on the reformatory. About eight hundred inmates resided there, all boys, all white, almost all Catholic, and ranging in age from five to twenty-one. Orphans were mixed with delinquents, truants with more serious offenders. On admission, George Ruth was officially classified as "incorrigible," which, strictly speaking, means "bad beyond reform; incapable of being corrected."

St. Mary's was run by the Catholic Order of Xaverian Brothers. The

Brothers took their inspiration from and professed to live according to the ideals and example of St. Francis Xavier, a sixteenth-century Jesuit missionary. The order was founded in Belgium in 1839 and from the beginning specialized, as it still does, in the teaching of disadvantaged children on the elementary and high school levels.

On the theory that Satan finds work for idle hands, St. Mary's made sure its residents were fully occupied and then some. Reveille at six in the morning was followed by compulsory attendance at mass before breakfast. Classroom instruction began at eight and continued until noon. After lunch came further classroom work or vocational training, under the supervision of the Brothers, until midafternoon. Two or three hours of organized outdoor recreation preceded dinner—official policy was for the boys to play outdoors at least two hours daily, weather permitting. Bedtime was early (lights out at eight!) in four dormitories of two hundred beds each.

Baseball was not the only recreational activity available, but it was certainly the most popular. The game was already the country's undisputed National Pastime, and, after all, the institution was located in turn-of-the-century Baltimore—home of the renowned Orioles, three-time pennant winners in the nineties. St. Mary's had several playing fields on its grounds and many teams grouped into various leagues. Some leagues were organized by dormitory, some by floor, some by age group, and so on. From March through October, intramural baseball competition was easily the hottest topic of conversation among the boys—and probably among the Brothers as well.

At first seven-year-old George was miserable in this highly structured and disciplined environment, having spent most of his life unconfined and uncontrolled. Even more painful must have been the knowledge that he had been abandoned by his mother and father. He was deeply hurt by the fact that in all the years he was at St. Mary's, which was most of his life to the age of nineteen, no member of his family ever came to visit him—no one came to visit on the one Sunday a month that visitors were allowed, no one came on holidays, no one even came at Christmastime. Apparently he never had a visitor of any kind, family or otherwise, during his lengthy confinement at the institution.

Louis Leisman, a classmate of Ruth's at St. Mary's, recalled George's usual reaction: "Well," he would say, "I guess I'm just too big and ugly for anyone to come see me. Maybe next Sunday."

As time went by, though, he began to feel more content. Indeed, in later years he would fondly and nostalgically recall the institution as his "real" childhood home. The main reason for his change of heart was that he fortunately found someone he could trust, respect, and try to emulate.

"It was at St. Mary's," he told writer Bob Considine in 1947, when they were working together on his autobiography, "that I met and learned to love the greatest man I've ever known. His name was Brother Matthias. He was the father I needed. He taught me to read and write—and he taught me the difference between right and wrong."

Brother Matthias was a giant of a man, six feet six inches tall, a well-muscled 250 pounds. No doubt because of his great size and strength, he was prefect of discipline at St. Mary's, in charge of keeping law and order among hundreds of closely confined, restless, volatile youngsters. George Ruth, of course, was no angel. A certified incorrigible at the age of seven, a troublemaker from way back, he ironically came to revere Brother Matthias, the embodiment of established authority; indeed, his admiration became so great that for a while George even thought about entering the priesthood himself.

Brother Matthias apparently accomplished his objectives without raising his voice and with a minimum of physical force. His appearance was

The recreation yard and main buildings of St. Mary's as they looked when George Ruth lived there.

so imposing, and his strength so celebrated, that none of his charges dared challenge his authority.

The story is told of an afternoon at St. Mary's when some older boys started a small riot in the yard that threatened to spread. Brother Matthias was hurriedly sent for. When he arrived he stood on some high ground in the yard and just looked out over the uprising, not moving a muscle, not saying a word. The yard immediately grew quiet and the fighting stopped.

"I think I was born as a hitter the first day I ever saw him hit a baseball," Ruth told Considine. "It was during the summer of 1902, my first year at St. Mary's. The baseball of that time was a lump of mush. But Brother Matthias would stand at the end of the yard, a finger mitt on his left hand and a bat in his right, toss the ball up with his left hand and give it a terrific belt with the bat he held in his right hand. When he felt like it, he could hit it a little harder and make the ball clear the fence in center field. The ball would have to carry at least 350 feet, a terrific knock in those days and a real sock—in view of the fact that it was hit with one hand—even today. I would stand there and watch him, bug-eyed."

Brother Matthias spent a disproportionate amount of time with the youngster, considering that about eight hundred others were also in his custody. He helped him with his schoolwork, talked with him about his future, and was always ready with support and encouragement.

He also played a critical role in developing and shaping young George Ruth's God-given raw baseball talent. He taught by practice and by repetition: by hitting baseballs to Ruth and others for hour after hour. George's natural ability was apparent at an early age. By the time he was eight or nine he was playing with the twelve-year-old team, when he was twelve he was competing with sixteen-year-olds, and at the age of sixteen he was on the varsity. "I could always hit," Ruth said in later years, "but it was Brother Matthias who made me a fielder."

He made him a pitcher, too. Ruth played just about any position, infield or outfield, but he liked catching best—he used a right-hander's catcher's mitt, even though he threw left-handed, because no other mitt was available. One afternoon in 1909 or 1910 a St. Mary's pitcher was getting hit hard and Ruth, who was catching, started laughing.

"What's so funny, George?" asked Brother Matthias.

"Nothing, sir."

"If you think it's so easy, George, let's see *you* pitch. Show us how it's done."

Thus George Ruth approached the mound reluctantly for the first time and, as fate would have it, shut out the opposition for the remainder of the game. Thereafter he pitched more often than he caught, but since he couldn't pitch every day he still went behind the plate frequently.

In 1912 the St. Mary's newspaper, *The Saturday Evening Star*, published an account of a game where George Ruth, then seventeen years old, batting leadoff, hit a home run, triple, and double, played third base, caught, and also pitched several innings, striking out six batters!

It was not Brother Matthias who actually paved the way for Ruth's entry into professional baseball, however. That honor goes to Brother Gilbert, baseball coach at nearby Mount St. Joseph's, sister institution of St. Mary's, who was of course familiar with Ruth's diamond prowess. Brother Gilbert contacted Jack Dunn, owner and manager of the Baltimore Orioles in the International League, and urged him to take a look at this youngster who performed wonders on a baseball diamond.

The Baltimore Orioles had been a major league powerhouse in the nineties, led by "Hit 'em where they ain't" Wee Willie Keeler and fiery John McGraw, one five feet four and the other a towering five feet seven. Baltimore won National League pennants in 1894, '95, and '96, and finished a strong second in '97 and '98.

However, an interleague financial war erupted at the turn of the century—the upstart American League versus the established National League—and in 1901 the Baltimore club joined the newly organized American League. Only two years later, though, the franchise was sold for $18,000 and transferred to New York. There the team was renamed the Highlanders; soon thereafter they would be called the Yankees, and subsequently they would close the circle by becoming rich and famous on the strong back of one George H. Ruth.

No longer a major league city in 1903, and not very happy about the demotion, Baltimore had no choice but to be satisfied with a consolation minor league franchise in the Eastern League (which changed its name to the International League in 1912). Jack Dunn, former journeyman big league pitcher and infielder and a well-known resident of Baltimore, was named the Orioles' manager in 1907. A couple of years later he bought the club, thereby becoming its owner as well. With the passage of time, Dunn acquired an enviable reputation as an astute judge of baseball talent and made a tidy living for two decades by developing young ballplayers with the Orioles and selling them to the big leagues. He hit the jackpot in 1924, when he sold future Hall of Famer Lefty Grove to the Philadelphia Athletics for $100,600, then a record sum for a minor leaguer.

This was the Jack Dunn who came to St. Mary's to see for himself what all the fuss was about. For the occasion, the schools arranged a special game—St. Mary's versus Mount St. Joseph's—to showcase the young star. George was at the top of his form, pitching St. Mary's to an 8–0 victory and striking out fourteen (or twenty-two, depending on which report you read). As a result, in February of 1914, shortly after Ruth's nineteenth birthday, Jack Dunn and St. Mary's Xaverian Brothers agreed on the terms of a contract between George Ruth and the Baltimore Orioles.

Although George's father was still alive, the Brothers were his legal guardians and by law he was supposed to remain at St. Mary's until he was twenty-one. This problem was taken care of by the formality of having Dunn assume Ruth's guardianship, with the Orioles' owner becoming accountable to Maryland courts for George's welfare until his twenty-first birthday. However, there is no indication that the owner ever lost any sleep over his newfound responsibility—indeed, strapped for cash, Dunn sold his young ward to the Boston Red Sox for $2,900 only five months later!

With respect to George's parents, his mother, who had been in poor health for many years, had passed away in 1910 at the age of thirty-four. His father died in 1918, at the age of forty-six, following a street brawl outside his saloon. Although many people think Ruth was orphaned as a young child because he grew up in St. Mary's, which was in part an orphanage, he did not actually become an orphan until 1918, when he was twenty-three.

Ruth's contract with the Orioles stipulated a salary of $600 for the season, or $100 a month, by no means a small amount back then. In 1914 a sumptuous dinner at elegant Churchill's (at Broadway and Forty-ninth Street in New York) cost all of $1.25; a luxury hotel room was $3.00 a night; and automobile manufacturer Henry Ford had just made the sensational announcement that he was going to pay his workers an unprecedented $5.00 a day, double the prevailing blue-collar wage.

Thus on February 27, 1914, almost twelve years after he had arrived, George Ruth, now six feet two and a broad-shouldered, flat-bellied 185 pounds, walked out of St. Mary's a free man, bound for spring training with the Orioles. "You'll make it, George," said Brother Matthias.

And someone, no one knows who, made a final handwritten entry next to the name George Herman Ruth, Jr., in the St. Mary's record book. It read, simply: "Discharged. He is going to join the Balt. Baseball Team."

On February 6, 1895, George Ruth, Jr., was born in this house at 216 Emory Street (second doorway from the left) in Baltimore, Maryland. He was born on the second floor in the front bedroom (second and third windows from the left).

Lamps and Oil.

(See Oil Dealers.)

Ammidon & Co. (kerosene oil and lamps) 347 w Baltimore and 60 German
Armor Geo. F. 164 Franklin
Baker George, 306 n Gay
Bangert Philip, s w cor Central av and Chew
Bakee Howard, 14 n Howard
Cosgrove Horatio G. 44 e Baltimore
Duff J. Luther, 49 Pearl
Erich Henry C. & Co. 77 Gough
Eisenhardt Anton, 254 n Gay
Grimes Charles E. 99 Lexington
Guthrie James W. 456 w Baltimore
Halle Philip (lamp fluid) 18 s Charles
Hamill & Co. 131 n Gay
Hitt Mrs. Christiana, 145 e Baltimore
Horton Mrs. Jane, 426 w Baltimore
Howard Charles, Baltimore nr Harrison
Jones Mrs. Catherine, 79 e Lombard
Kraft Conrad & Son, 62 n Eutaw
Lange Ralph, 68 n Howard
Mowbray & Co. 2 e Baltimore
O'Laughlin Mrs. Emma, 17 Orleans
Schaefer Henry, 690 w Baltimore
Scheier Joseph, 217 s Broadway
Schminke Henry, 690 w Baltimore
Spilcker Wm. & H. 136 w Baltimore

Last Makers.

Marshall John L. 59 n Frederick
Merriken Joseph S. cor Grant and Mercer

Laundries.

Baltimore Maryland Laundry, Annie Clark, proprietress, rear 107 w Baltimore
Baltimore Steam Laundry, 4 s High
Bentz George W. 131 w Baltimore
Richardson Edward T. over n e cor Baltimore and Frederick
Search Christopher, 4 s High
Search N. C. & Co. 476 w Baltimore

Leather Belting.

Haskell John H. 33 s Eutaw

Leather and Oil Dealers.

(See Curriers.)

Achey Frederick & Son, 22 s Liberty

Ott George L. 36 e Pratt
Roque Francis, cor Fayette and Harrison
Rose Bros. 60 s Calvert
Scally & Anderson, 44 Light
Sharp & Malloy, cor Balderston and Grant
Stehli Anthony, 175 s Bond
Weinrich Frederick, 477 w Baltimore

Lightning Rods.

Bishop Caleb, 51 Ensor
Bishop John H. 81 n High
McLain James, Sun building, South

Lime.

Auld Haddaway, 31 n Greene
Bowen & Mercer, 65 s Gay
Coburn Solomon, 30 Concord
Costello John, (kilns) Fayette e of Burke
Cunningham & Ditman, cor Forrest and Monument
Diggs Richd. H. & Sons, 258 s Caroline
Distler John C. cor Chester and Canton av
Dorsey John & Son, (kilns) cor Castle and Orleans

LEFT: Young George's father eventually became a full-time saloonkeeper, but for a while he worked in the family lightning-rod business that had been founded by *his* father, John A. Ruth. It was located at 228 South Sharp Street in Baltimore.

BELOW: The only known photograph showing young George with his mother. The picture was taken at a family gathering in the summer of 1896. Kate Ruth and her year-and-a-half-old son are in the first row at the far left. She is supporting him with her right arm, her left hand unobtrusively making sure he looks in the camera's direction.

The main entrance of St. Mary's Industrial School for Boys as it looked when it was George Ruth's home. The Wilkens Avenue trolley-car tracks ran from downtown Baltimore directly past the front door.

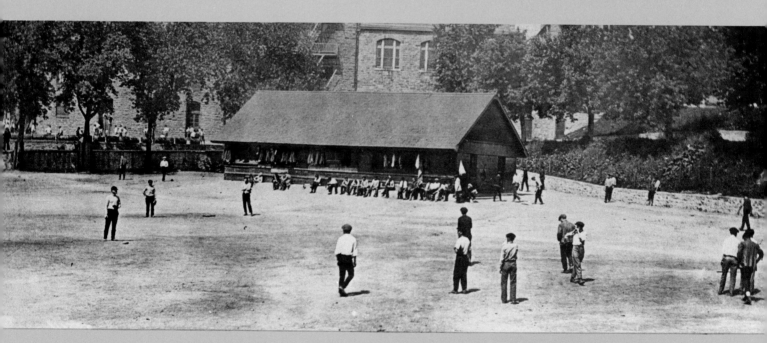

The playgrounds and ball fields behind the main buildings, where Brother Matthias used to hit fungoes and George Ruth learned to play baseball.

Two pals shortly after the turn of the century. On the right is George Ruth, Jr., age seven, soon after he was committed to St. Mary's in 1902. The youngster on the left, leaning on the bat, is one of Ruth's friends at St. Mary's, John DeTullio.

Brother Matthias: "The greatest man I've ever known."

ABOVE: The tailor shop at St. Mary's. Because of the vocational education he received, if George hadn't become a ballplayer he probably would have ended up as a pretty good tailor. His special training was in shirtmaking.

RIGHT: The year is 1911 and George Ruth is the star of the St. Mary's varsity. Here he is at shortstop.

George Ruth, father and son, looked so much alike they could be mistaken as twins. Here the Babe (second from right, his left arm partially obscured by the punch bowl), in his early twenties, helps tend bar in his father's saloon during the Christmas season. George Sr. is on the right. The year is 1915 or 1916.

George was also St. Mary's number one catcher. He threw lefty, but no left-hander's catcher's mitts were available, so he had to make do with a right-hander's glove.

RIGHT: The winners of St. Mary's schoolwide championships around 1910 to 1912. In the photo of eight players, Ruth is in the center. On the upper left is Fritz Maisel, who also made it to the big leagues. Maisel played second and third base for the Yankees in the teens. In the other photo, the left-handed catcher standing in the back row wants to make the position he plays perfectly clear. Ruth is wearing his chest protector and proudly displaying both his catcher's mask and (right-hander's) mitt.

23

A nattily dressed nineteen-year-old George Herman Ruth signs a contract to play ball with Baltimore in 1914. Owner Jack Dunn is seated at his desk; looking over Ruth's shoulder is Ned Hanlon, previous owner of the Baltimore Orioles.

Jack Dunn, the legendary manager and owner of the Baltimore Orioles from 1907 to 1928.

A savage fire devastated St. Mary's in 1919.

In 1920 Babe Ruth escorted the school's band from city to city around the
American League, seeking donations to rebuild the institution. Here they are

at Shibe Park, Philadelphia, with the band ready to play before a regularly scheduled game between the Yankees and Athletics.

The Best Left-handed Pitcher in Baseball

1914-1918

The Baltimore Orioles trained in Fayetteville, North Carolina, in the spring of 1914. Although there are several versions of how Ruth got his nickname, the most widely accepted account is his own: "On the first day of spring training, Dunn practically led me by the hand from the dressing room to the pitcher's box. I was as proud of my Orioles' uniform as I had been of my first long pants. Maybe I showed that pride in my face and the way I walked. 'Look at Dunnie and his new babe,' yelled one of the older players" (according to legend, it was coach Sam Steinman).

"Babe"—it stuck because it was a natural for Ruth. He had spent all his life behind institutional walls, and even the most ordinary things—railroad trains, elevators, restaurants, money in any amount above small change—were sources of wonder to the wide-eyed nineteen-year-old.

"Why, he's just a babe in the woods," someone said one evening, watching him ride up and down in the hotel elevator because it was so much fun.

By the time the Orioles began moving north to open the season, his teammates, newspapermen, and the fans were all calling him either "Baby" or "Babe." "Baby" didn't last long, but "Babe" never left him for the rest of his life.

Ruth had a sensational spring. From the beginning, there never was any question about his ability to make the team as a regular pitcher. He threw like a professional the first time he stepped on the pitcher's mound. And at bat his screaming line drives and long booming fly balls became a leading topic of conversation in Fayetteville. Opponents and teammates alike, along with the fans, oohed and aahed at how high and far he hit the ball, just the way the kids had at St. Mary's. Even veteran ballplayers agreed they'd never seen anything like it.

Part of the reason was his swing. Instead of place hitting—choking up on the bat and trying to punch ground balls between the infielders or trying to hit line drives between the outfielders, the typical batting style in those dead-ball days—Ruth did exactly the opposite. A left-handed batter, he held his bat down at the very end, reared back, and swung from his heels with all his might. Swinging for the fences is commonplace nowadays, but in 1914 it was contrary to the accepted axioms of proper "scientific" hitting.

He hit his first home run with the Orioles in the very first intrasquad game of the spring. The ball cleared the right field fence and landed in a cornfield. "I hit it as I hit all the others," he reminisced many years later, "by taking a good gander at the pitch as it came up to the plate, twisting my body into a backswing, and then hitting it as hard as I could swing."

When he missed, which was fairly often, he'd lose his balance and almost fall down because he'd swung so hard. That caused as much talk as if he'd connected.

But he was still mainly a pitcher, not a hitter, and it was as a left-handed pitcher that he made the Baltimore team in 1914. He had good control and a lively fastball that naturally tailed away from right-handed batters. Although his curve was excellent, while at St. Mary's he acquired the unconscious habit of curling his tongue in the corner of his mouth when throwing it. He didn't break the habit, he recalled years later, "until Bill Carrigan, my first big league manager, convinced me that I was 'telegraphing' every curve with my tongue."

It is not possible to say exactly what the speed of Ruth's fastball was, since there was no radar gun in those days to measure the speed of a pitched ball. On the basis of comments by his contemporaries, however, a reasonable guess would put it in the neighborhood of 90 miles an hour. His fastball was his best pitch and he was often mentioned in the same breath with Walter Johnson, the fastest pitcher of the era, possibly the fastest of all time. As an aside, Ruth and Johnson opposed each other as starting pitchers eight times in the four years from 1915 through 1918; Ruth won *six* of the eight games, three of them by scores of 1–0.

He needed seasoning, of course, but he was already a surprisingly accomplished pitcher in that first spring training camp at Fayetteville. Witness Ben Egan, the Orioles' catcher: "It would be pleasant to say that I developed Ruth as a pitcher, but that would be hogwash. He knew how to pitch the first day I saw him. He knew how to hold runners on base and he knew how to work on the hitters. I didn't have to tell him anything."

Ruth's professional pitching debut took place on April 22, 1914, on the second day of the season, when he walked cockily out to the pitcher's mound in Baltimore, his hometown, to face the visiting Buffalo Bisons. Oddly enough, the second batter up was Buffalo's second baseman, Joe McCarthy—the same Joe McCarthy who sixteen years later would get the job Ruth wanted, manager of the New York Yankees. At the time, though, McCarthy was just another good-field/no-hit infielder who would never make the big leagues as a player. Ruth shut out Buffalo with only six hits and got two singles himself, as Baltimore won easily, 6–0.

By early July, young Babe Ruth—the name was already catching on—had 14 wins and 6 losses and had won eight of his last nine decisions. His ability established, Dunn doubled his annual pay to $1,200 in May and raised it again to $1,800 in June. Ruth was flabbergasted: in February he was sleeping in a dorm with two hundred other kids, lucky to have a nickel in his pocket, and now barely six months later and he was not only famous but rich too!

He was also becoming quite a traveler: Montreal, Toronto, Buffalo, Rochester, Providence, Jersey City, Newark—all were in the International League and he was a celebrity in each. Well, maybe not a full-fledged celebrity, not yet, but plenty of people *did* seem to know him wherever he went. Train rides, dining cars, restaurants, hotels (and hotel elevators!)—not to mention, most important of all, playing baseball every single day. After so many years of being cooped up in St. Mary's, with walls and guards and gates and rules, he could hardly believe it wasn't all a crazy dream.

For Jack Dunn, the 1914 season had also turned into a dream—in his case, though, it was a nightmare. His Baltimore Orioles were leading the International League and he had, he thought, the league's top gate attraction in the bargain. But no one in Baltimore seemed to give a damn. All the fans were in the *other* ballpark across the street, cheering the brand-new Baltimore Terrapins in the brand-new Federal League—in the brand-new *major* league.

Baltimore had never forgiven the baseball establishment for bumping the Orioles out of the American League in 1903 and dumping them into the minors. The residents of Maryland's premier city did not think of Baltimore as a minor league town, and their resentment had not diminished. If anything, it had intensified. So when an "outlaw" league—the Federal League—began operating in 1914, and called itself a third major league, Baltimore fans flocked to see the "big league" Baltimore Terrapins and ignored the minor league Orioles.

Attendance at many Orioles' games was less than a hundred. Sometimes only about fifteen or twenty lonely fans were scattered through the stands. By contrast, attendance was thriving at Federal League games. The difference was especially striking because the Terrapins built their new ballpark directly across the street from Dunn's International League park. Tens of thousands walked right past Oriole Park on their way to see the Terrapins play.

The financial pressures on Jack Dunn became so great that he could no longer meet his payroll and had no choice but to sell off his best players at cut-rate prices. Thus on July 8 he sold Ruth, another young pitcher, Ernie Shore, and catcher Ben Egan to the Boston Red Sox for a sum reported at the time to be $8,500, of which $2,900 was said to be for George Herman Ruth, Jr.

This meant still another pay raise for Ruth, since soon after he reported to Boston his annual salary was almost doubled, to $3,500—close to six times what he had started at in February. For this figure, he agreed to a two-and-a-half-year contract, carrying through 1916.

On July 11, 1914, Babe Ruth made his major league debut: he took the mound in Fenway Park for the Boston Red Sox against the Cleveland Indians. Although he needed relief help in the last two innings, he was the winning pitcher by a score of 4–3. Apparently Boston Manager Bill Carrigan was not too impressed, however, because he hardly used him again in the next month. To Ruth's disappointment, he was sent back to the International League in August, this time to the Providence club, an affiliate of the Red Sox.

With Providence, he won 8 and lost 3, giving him a 22–9 record for the season in the International League. He also hit his first professional home run, on September 5, in a game against Toronto that he won by pitching a one-hit shutout.

But the end of the baseball season was only a milestone on the express track of this unbelievable year for the kid from St. Mary's.

"I felt rich enough and old enough," he said in his autobiography, "to take to myself a wife. She was Helen Woodring, who came originally from Nova Scotia and was a waitress at Landers' Coffee Shop in Boston when I first met her. She used to wait on me in the mornings, and one day I said to her, 'How about you and me getting married, hon?' Helen thought it over for a few minutes and said yes."

Oh well, Babe never could remember names! The young woman who became his wife in October of 1914, after they had known each other only three months, was Helen Wood*ford*, a pretty, petite, seventeen-year-old brunette. She was shy, reserved, quiet, ill-at-ease in the public eye, a true homebody—in other words, she was the exact opposite of her husband. Although the marriage lasted legally for fifteen years, only the first few were happy. Thereafter, despite the best of intentions, the more famous Babe became, the more they drifted apart.

Ruth was a regular on the Boston Red Sox in 1915, a full-fledged starter on Manager Bill Carrigan's pitching staff. The Red Sox were no ordinary team. This was essentially the same ball club that had won the pennant and the World Series in 1912, had finished second in 1914, and was poised to win pennants (and the World Series as well) in 1915, '16, and '18. Four World Championships in seven years. Especially celebrated was the outfield of Harry Hooper in right field, Tris Speaker in center, and Duffy Lewis in left. Some still maintain that they formed the best defensive outfield of all time.

The Red Sox didn't know quite how to react to this brash kid from the Baltimore waterfront. His talk and actions were so coarse that he even startled professional athletes, men who had more than a passing acquaintance with some pretty boorish behavior.

Fellow pitcher Ernie Shore, for example, was assigned as Ruth's roommate on road trips, probably because they had been teammates in Baltimore. But after a few weeks he went to Manager Carrigan and asked for a change. "He uses my toothbrush," complained Shore.

"Well, so what?" was Ruth's response. "He's welcome to use mine if he wants to."

He also ate enormous quantities of food, mostly junk food, and didn't seem to have the vaguest idea about such things as diet and health, not to mention the most elementary of table manners. Outfielder Harry Hooper was an established star on the Red Sox when Ruth arrived. "He had never been anywhere," Hooper recalled. "He didn't even know anything about manners or how to behave among people. And Lord, he ate too much. He'd stop along the road when we were traveling and order half a dozen hot dogs and as many bottles of soda pop, stuff them in, one after the other, and then give a few big belches. That would hold him for a couple of hours and then he'd be at it again. 'You better be careful, Babe,' I warned him one day, when he was gorging himself like that. 'Careful about what?' he asked.

"His behavior was so crude that he got more than his share of teasing, some of it not too pleasant. 'The big baboon' a lot of them used to call him behind his back—or 'the big monkey' or 'the big ape'—and then a few got up enough nerve to ridicule him to his face. This started to get under his skin, and when they didn't let up he finally challenged the whole ball club. Nobody was so dumb as to take him up on it, so that put an end to mimicking him to his face. But they continued to make fun of him behind his back."

The reason no one would accept Ruth's challenge was because of his size and strength. He was often referred to as "the big guy" or "the big fellow" because he *was* big. In 1915, at the age of twenty, he was six feet two and weighed a well-proportioned muscular 198 pounds, a good four inches taller and 25 pounds heavier than the average major leaguer of that era.

Ruth had 18 wins against 8 losses in 1915, with a 2.44 earned run average. He also hit 4 home runs. His first big league homer—a drive into the right field stands—came on May 6 against the Yankees' Jack Warhop in the Polo Grounds, which the Yankees then shared with the New York Giants. Four home runs don't sound like a lot today, but in 1915 the grand total for the rest of the Boston team was only 10. The league leader that year, Braggo Roth, had 7.

The following two years saw Babe Ruth come into his own as a pitcher. He was a twenty-game winner in both years, 23–12 in 1916 and 24–13 in 1917, with earned run averages of 1.75 in 1916 and 2.02 in 1917. He led the American League in earned run average and shutouts (9) in 1916, and in complete games (35) in 1917.

In the 1916 World Series he won one game, a fourteen-inning 2–1 affair, in which he allowed the opposition a run in the first inning and then shut them out for thirteen innings thereafter. In the 1918 World Series he won two more, by scores of 1–0 and 3–2. In the latter game, the opposition didn't score until the eighth inning, giving Ruth a pitching record of 29⅔ consecutive scoreless World Series innings, a record that stood for forty-three years. The record Ruth broke had been held by the great Christy Mathewson—28⅓ consecutive scoreless World Series innings.

There is no question but that Ruth was the best left-handed pitcher in baseball at the time. Not the best pitcher, period: that honor would have to go to either Walter Johnson of the American League or Grover Cleveland Alexander of the National League, both of whom were right-handed.

Ruth's only serious rival as the best left-hander in the game was Jim "Hippo" Vaughn of the Chicago Cubs, who was called "Hippo" because he was six feet four and weighed 215 pounds. Vaughn earned a place in baseball history on May 2, 1917, when he and Fred Toney of Cincinnati *both* pitched no-hitters through nine innings. (Toney won in the tenth, when Vaughn allowed two hits and the game's only run.) Just as Ruth beat Walter Johnson repeatedly in their man-to-man matchups, so he won the only game he and Vaughn ever pitched against each other—it was the first game of the 1918 World Series and the final score was Red Sox 1–Cubs 0.

Along with sudden success, however, came more than a little arrogance, insolence, and the throwing of temper tantrums, an unfortunate extension of the cockiness that had always been part of Ruth's makeup. It reached a peak on June 23, 1917, when he toed Fenway Park's pitching rubber against the Washington Senators. Behind the plate, umpire Brick Owens called Ruth's first four pitches balls and waved the batter to first base—as a result of which Ruth lost all semblance of self-control. He rushed off the pitching mound and, after a brief nose-to-nose shouting match, hauled off and punched the umpire with a solid left hook (although some witnesses claim he missed with the left and landed a follow-up right).

In any event, "it wasn't a love pat; I really socked him—right on the jaw."

The incident had a stunning sequel. Ernie Shore replaced Ruth (who was thrown out of the game) and proceeded to retire twenty-six consecutive batters. The leadoff man was thrown out trying to steal second base and no other Washington batter was able to reach first. Consequently, since then Shore's name has been included on the select list of pitchers who have hurled not just a no-hit game but a perfect no-hit game.

Ban Johnson, American League president, fined Ruth a hundred dollars and suspended him for ten days, surprisingly mild punishment given the nature of the offense. Ruth apologized for his behavior and vowed that he had learned his lesson.

Best left-hander in the game though he might be, he was destined to abandon the pitching mound shortly. Because in addition to a 2.22 earned-run average in 1918, he also batted .300 and hit 11 homers—tying Philadelphia Athletics' outfielder Tilly Walker for the most home runs in the major leagues that year.

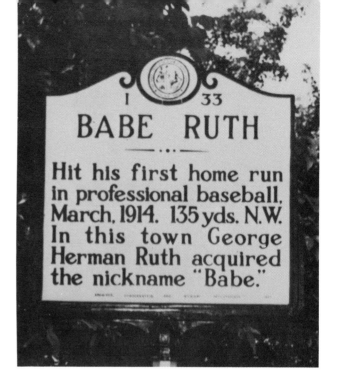

Marker in Fayetteville, North Carolina, commemorating the spot where Babe Ruth hit his first home run (into a cornfield, in spring training with the Baltimore Orioles). His first home run in an official league game came in Toronto on September 5, 1914. His first major league homer was hit off Jack Warhop of the New York Yankees on May 6, 1915.

The 1914 Baltimore Orioles. Ruth is on the far right, leaning on Ben Egan. Next comes Jack Dunn, with his arm around his son, Jack Jr. On young Jack's right is

Ben Egan, Ruth's catcher with the
Baltimore Orioles in 1914. A skillful
catcher, Egan spent most of his career in
the minor leagues because of weak
hitting.

infielder Neal Ball, who will be forever remembered as the first man to make an
unassisted triple play in the major leagues (he did it while playing shortstop for
Cleveland in 1909).

RUTH
PITCHER

ABOVE: Babe Ruth as a rookie with the Baltimore Orioles in 1914.

Joseph J. Lannin. He bought the Boston Red Sox in 1913 and bought Babe Ruth from Jack Dunn in 1914. The Sox thereupon won two World Series, in 1915 and 1916, but late in 1916 he sold the club to Harry Frazee anyway.

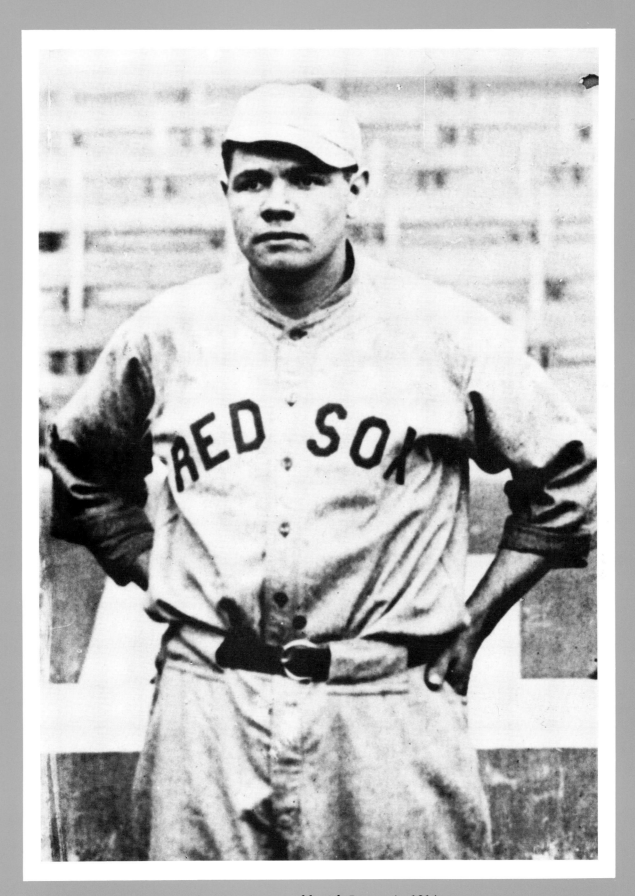

A nineteen-year-old with Boston in 1914.

Ruth pitched well with the Red Sox in 1914, but in August he was back in the minors, this time with the Providence Grays. His 1914 pitching record with Baltimore and Providence in the International League was 22 wins and 9 losses.

As a teenager, the Babe loved bicycles. At spring training with Baltimore in 1914, the sight of Ruth careening down the street on a borrowed bicycle was enough to send pedestrians rushing for cover.

BELOW: Center fielder Tris Speaker (left) and pitcher Smoky Joe Wood were established stars on the Boston Red Sox when Ruth joined the team in 1914. They were not amused by the cocky rookie's boisterous behavior and lack of respect.

Boston's Fenway Park as it looked when Ruth was with the Red Sox, from 1914 through 1919.

LEFT: The Boston Red Sox in spring training in 1915. The Red Sox became the World Champions that year, so perhaps the steamroller on which they are posing is appropriate. In the photo are: (1) A fan, (2) Forrest Cady, (3) Chet Thomas (4) Groundkeeper, (5) Smoky Joe Wood, (6) Carl Mays, (7) Germany Schaefer, (8) A fan, (9) Vean Gregg, (10) A fan, 11) A fan, (12) Hooks Dauss, (13) Dutch Leonard, (14) Babe Ruth, (15) Rube Foster (16) Guy Cooper, (17) Charlie Flanagan, (18) Heinie Wagner, (19) Ray Collins, (20) Ray Haley, (21) Rip Hagerman, (22) Joe Lannin (owner), (23) Bill Carrigan (manager), (24) Bill Sweeney, (25) Ernie Shore.

The year is 1915 and Manager Bill Carrigan of the Red Sox is receiving an award. Pitcher Ernie Shore and owner Joe Lannin watch the proceedings from behind Carrigan, with pitcher Babe Ruth an equally interested spectator.

Four pitching mainstays of the 1915 and 1916 World Champion Boston Red Sox. Left to right: Ernie Shore, Dutch Leonard, Rube Foster, and Babe Ruth.

Six-foot-four Ernie Shore was sold by Baltimore to the Red Sox in 1914, along with Ben Egan and Babe Ruth. One day in 1917 he relieved Ruth on the pitching mound, after Babe had walked the first batter in the first inning, and proceeded to pitch no less than a perfect game.

LEFT TO RIGHT: Ed Barrow, ballplayer-turned-evangelist Billy Sunday, and Ruth.

On the Red Sox bench at a spring exhibition game. Ruth is fourth from the left.

Tyrus Raymond Cobb, king of the dead-ball era. He does not realize it yet, but his reign will soon come to a sudden end (because the dead ball will soon be extinct).

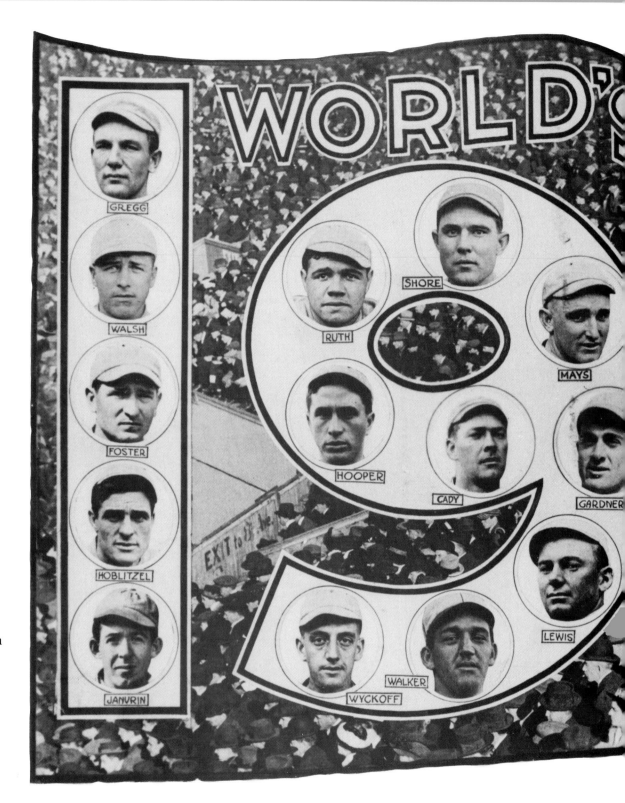

The Boston Red Sox won their second World Series in a row in 1916. They would win again in 1918, and thereafter enter a very long period of deprivation.

CHAMPIONS

THOMAS

SCOTT

GAINER

HENDRICKSEN

WAGNER

CARRIGAN

BARRY

JONES

McNALLY

LEONARD

SHORTEN

AGNEW

The best left-handed
pitcher in baseball.

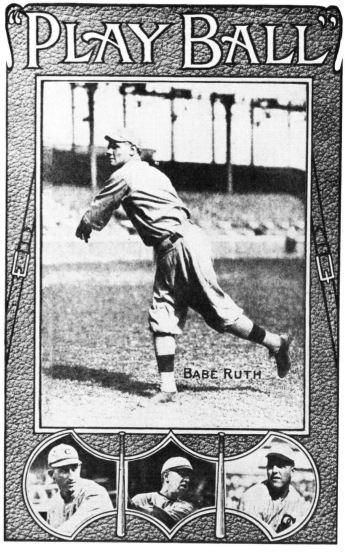

SLIM SALLEE   EDDIE COLLINS   EDDIE CICOTTE

But it was his hitting
that seized the
imagination of the fans.

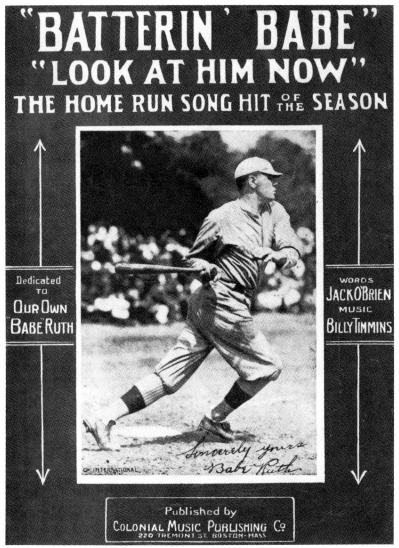

ABOVE: Hall of Famer Harry Hooper, the person most responsible for transforming Ruth from a pitcher into an outfielder. Hooper convinced Red Sox management that Ruth's bat should be in the lineup every day rather than only one day out of four or five.

Ruth and Red Sox pitcher Herb Pennock (on the right). Pennock came from a wealthy patrician family and had ridden horses for sport all his life. Ruth's background was somewhat different. Nevertheless, they became lifelong friends.

While with the Red Sox, Babe became part owner of a small Boston cigar factory that manufactured the Babe Ruth cigar. He even learned how to roll them himself.

THE BOSTO
LAWLER MILLER JONES THOMAS RUTH HOOP
SCOTT DUBUC BUSH WHITEMAN
MAS

ED SOX 1918
YS SHEAN KINNEY STRUNK McINNIS BARROW
ANG MAYER WAGNER AGNEW COFFEY
BATBOY

Mr. and Mrs. Babe Ruth in the early years of their marriage. It was July of 1914 when Helen Woodford, a seventeen-year-old waitress at Landers' Coffee Shop in Boston, met nineteen-year-old Babe Ruth, less than five months out of St. Mary's. Shortly thereafter, on October 17, the teenagers were married in St. Paul's Catholic Church in Ellicott City, Maryland, a suburb of Baltimore.

The House That Ruth Built

1919-1923

Ownership and management began changing on the Boston Red Sox soon after the World Championship 1916 season. By 1918 the New Order had been put in place and was in full operation: it consisted of Harry Frazee as the new owner and Ed Barrow as manager. They would play a crucial role in shaping the course of George Herman Ruth's career—and thereby, although they could hardly know it, in determining the future direction of the entire National Pastime.

H. Harrison Frazee was a fast-talking New York theatrical producer who took a flier on the Red Sox as though a ball club was just another musical comedy. In the seven years he owned the team, Frazee sold off all its stars in order to raise money to finance his stage ventures. He did have one big Broadway hit that made him millions, *No, No, Nanette!*, a 1925 musical in which the featured song was the still-popular "Tea for Two." By then, though, he was gone from Boston, where he'd left an empty shell in his wake.

Edward Grant Barrow was a longtime minor league manager and executive who most recently had been president of the International League. He was a crusty, hard-boiled autocrat, solidly built and quick with his dukes, who wouldn't take back talk from anybody. Although he was the manager and ostensibly directed the game from the bench, Barrow was more interested in front office matters, so that he left many of the field decisions to veteran outfielder and team captain Harry Hooper.

The 1918 season was the last in which Ruth was primarily a pitcher, with outfield and pinch-hitting duties on the side. In 1919 the balance shifted and Ruth became mainly an outfielder, pitching only occasionally. He appeared as a pitcher in only 17 games in 1919 and finished with 9 wins and 5 losses. Thereafter, he never pitched more than one or two games a year, and those mostly for fun or as an end-of-season gimmick to hype the gate.

For a month or two in 1919 Ruth was both an outfielder *and* a pitcher. After a while he complained to Barrow.

"Manager," he said (he invariably addressed Barrow as "Manager"), "I don't think I can keep on playing the outfield when I'm not pitching. It tires me out too much."

"If you'd cut down on your night life" was Barrow's answer, "you wouldn't tire so quickly."

Since it really was too much to expect Ruth to be a full-time outfielder and also take his regular pitching turn, a choice had to be made. Ruth himself expressed a preference for the outfield because he loved to hit, but Barrow was reluctant to lose the league's best left-hander. The balance was tipped when Hooper sided with Ruth.

"I finally convinced Ed Barrow to play him in the outfield," recalled Hooper fifty years later, "in order to get his bat in the lineup every day. Well, Ruth might have been a natural as a pitcher and as a hitter, but he sure wasn't a born outfielder. I was playing center field myself, so I put the Babe in right field. On the other side of me was a fellow named Braggo Roth, another wild man. I'd be playing out there in the middle between those two fellows and I began to fear for my life. Both of them were galloping around that outfield without regard for life or limb, hollering all the time, running like maniacs after every ball. A week of that was enough for me. I shifted the Babe to center and I moved to right, so I could keep clear of those two."

Once he settled into his new role, Ruth's booming bat more than justified the switch. In city after city he rocketed his patented sky-high home runs spectacular distances. The ball was still as dead as a mushy cantaloupe, but you couldn't prove it by the Babe. He homered in every park in the league in 1919, an unheard-of feat at the time, and set distance records in most. Excited crowds cheered his every move. He was a happening! The fans might "root, root, root for the home team," but more than anything they rooted for Babe Ruth to "hit one," even if he beat the home team when he did.

The twenty-four-year-old Ruth, of course, loved every minute of it. Life had never been better. His salary had moved up to $5,000 a year in 1917 and $7,000 in 1918. In March of 1919 he signed a new three-year contract with Frazee for $10,000 a year. He and Helen bought a nice country house and farm in Sudbury, Massachusetts, twenty miles west of Boston, and when the team was home, that's where he dutifully went after the game.

On the road, however, Babe was hard to fence in. An oft-told tale concerns an incident in Washington in 1919, when he sneaked into the Raleigh Hotel, where the team was staying, at six in the morning. Barrow, who had paid a hotel porter to let him know as soon as Ruth got in, promptly knocked on Ruth's door.

"Yes?"

Barrow opened the door to find Ruth lying in bed, blanket up to his chin, calmly puffing on a pipe.

"What are you doing smoking a pipe at this hour?" he roared.

"Oh, I do it all the time. I wake up in the middle of the night and have a few puffs. It helps me relax and get back to sleep," replied Ruth.

Barrow strode over to the bed and yanked off the blanket to find Ruth fully dressed, shoes and all. He looked at him scornfully. "You're a fine citizen, Babe, a fine citizen. That's all I have to say." And he stormed out.

That afternoon Ruth sought Barrow out in the locker room and gave him a piece of his mind. "If you ever barge into my room like that again," Ruth shouted, "I swear I'll knock your block off."

One thing led to another until Barrow challenged Ruth to a fight right then and there. Ruth was twenty-four and in perfect shape, Barrow fifty and out of condition. After a moment's hesitation, Ruth walked out of the locker room and onto the playing field. "And you can take that uniform off, too," Barrow yelled after him, "because you're suspended."

That evening a contrite Ruth knocked at Barrow's door to apologize. After a long lecture, in which the manager warned his young star about the perils of fast women and slow horses, a penitent Ruth tried to make up.

"Manager, if I leave a note in your box when I get in every night, and put the exact time on it, will that be all right with you? Then can I play?"

"Can I believe your notes, Babe?"

"Yes you can, Manager."

There was no more trouble. Without fail, Ruth left a note in Barrow's hotel mailbox every night on every road trip. He had an incongruously graceful handwriting, no doubt due to innumerable hours of penmanship practice at St. Mary's. The notes would be addressed "Dear Manager" or sometimes, inexplicably, "Dear Eddie," and they'd read: "I got back at eleven-thirty" or "two minutes before midnight" or whenever, and they were always signed "Babe."

Barrow said he never tried to verify their accuracy.

Despite his crazy hours, there was no letup in Ruth's home run barrage against American League pitchers. At first it was believed that the single-season home run record was 25, hit by Buck Freeman in 1899. The Babe tied and passed that mark in early September.

Then someone discovered that Ned Williamson of the Chicago White Stockings had hit 27 way back in 1884, when Chicago's Lakefront Park measured only 180 feet to the left field foul pole and 196 feet to the right field foul pole, the shortest major league outfield distances ever. He tied Williamson on September 20 and set a new record four days later. Ruth's final numbers for 1919 were 29 home runs, 114 runs batted in, 103 runs scored, all league-leading figures, and a .322 batting average. And to Harry Hooper's amazement, he even led the league's outfielders in *fielding* average!

But theatrical mogul Harry Frazee was in a financial bind. His stage ventures weren't paying off and he needed cash. To get it, he started selling players, mostly to the New York Yankees. Among those he sold to New York in 1919 and thereafter were pitchers Joe Bush, Waite Hoyt, Sam Jones, Carl Mays, Herb Pennock, and George Pipgras, catcher Wally Schang, shortstop Everett Scott, and third baseman Joe Dugan.

Also George Herman Ruth.

The big-shot theatrical promoter had the hottest show-biz ticket of the Roaring Twenties in his vest pocket, the greatest drawing card of the century, maybe the top box-office smash hit of all time—and in his infinite wisdom he practically gave him away. The sale price was $125,000; plus Yankee owner Colonel Jacob Ruppert agreed to personally lend $300,000 to Frazee (with the loan secured by a lien on Boston's Fenway Park). The transaction was consummated on December 26, 1919, and made public eleven days later, on January 6, 1920.

At that time, the Yankees had never won a pennant in their history and the Red Sox had won four World Championships in just the previous eight years. In the next thirteen years the Yankees won seven pennants (and four World Championships), while the Red Sox nose-dived into the American League cellar. In fact, a case can be made that to this very day the effects of that transaction are still rippling through both New York and New England: the Red Sox, after all, haven't won a World Series since 1918!

The Babe was playing golf in California when the deal was made. Yankee Manager Miller Huggins was quickly dispatched to the West Coast to tell him prior to the public announcement. Huggins, once a second baseman, was a little fellow, a skinny five feet six, who seemed even smaller because he was always being photographed next to beefy catchers and broad-shouldered first basemen.

After informing Ruth that he was now a Yankee, Huggins launched into a sermon on the temptations of the big city and the need for forbearance, temperance, and self-restraint. Ruth had never been much impressed with Huggins to begin with and anyway he'd heard that song before; indeed, he was so familiar with the lyrics that he could have given Huggins a few pointers about phrasing and joined him in the chorus. So he ignored the lecture and instead got straight to the heart of the matter: "Listen, Mr. Huggins, if Ruppert wants me on the Yankees you tell him he'll have to tear up that $10,000-a-year contract and give me a new one for $20,000."

Ruth also wanted a percentage of the purchase price, which he did not get, but he *did* manage to double his annual salary to $20,000, a successful outcome to the first of his many salary squabbles with Colonel Jacob Ruppert over the next decade and a half.

Exactly ten days after the sale was announced, the Eighteenth Amendment to the U.S. Constitution went into effect—the amendment that prohibited the manufacture, sale, and transportation of alcoholic beverages.

However, in spring training that year, at Jacksonville, the rambunctious New Yorkers acted as though they'd never heard of Prohibition. On one trip to Miami, to play the Cincinnati Reds, outfielder Ping Bodie got so soused he insisted on going to sleep when everybody else was getting up. It took four Yankees to carry the 200-pounder to the train that was to take the team to Palm Beach for another exhibition game.

Ruth got to the train on his own, but in Palm Beach, still feeling the effects of the night before, while chasing a fly ball he ran right into a palm tree that was planted in fair territory deep in the outfield, and knocked himself out.

Free of Ed Barrow and in no mood to pay attention to tiny Miller Huggins, Ruth turned every night into a celebration. Indeed, this was the spring when Ping Bodie (born Francesco Pezzolo), who was assigned to room with Ruth, came up with the classic line that was destined to long outlive its author. A reporter, hoping to get an inside story, asked Bodie what Ruth was really like.

"I've no idea," replied Bodie.

"What do you mean?" the reporter asked. "I thought you room with Babe Ruth."

"No," said Bodie, "I room with Babe Ruth's suitcase."

When the Yankees checked into a hotel, Ruth would soon be out on the town looking up old girlfriends or meeting new ones. Sometimes he'd return to the hotel briefly, and then off he'd go again. When it was time to check out, the agreeable Bodie would obligingly carry Ruth's bag back down to the hotel lobby.

Although he burned the candle at both ends, the life-style apparently

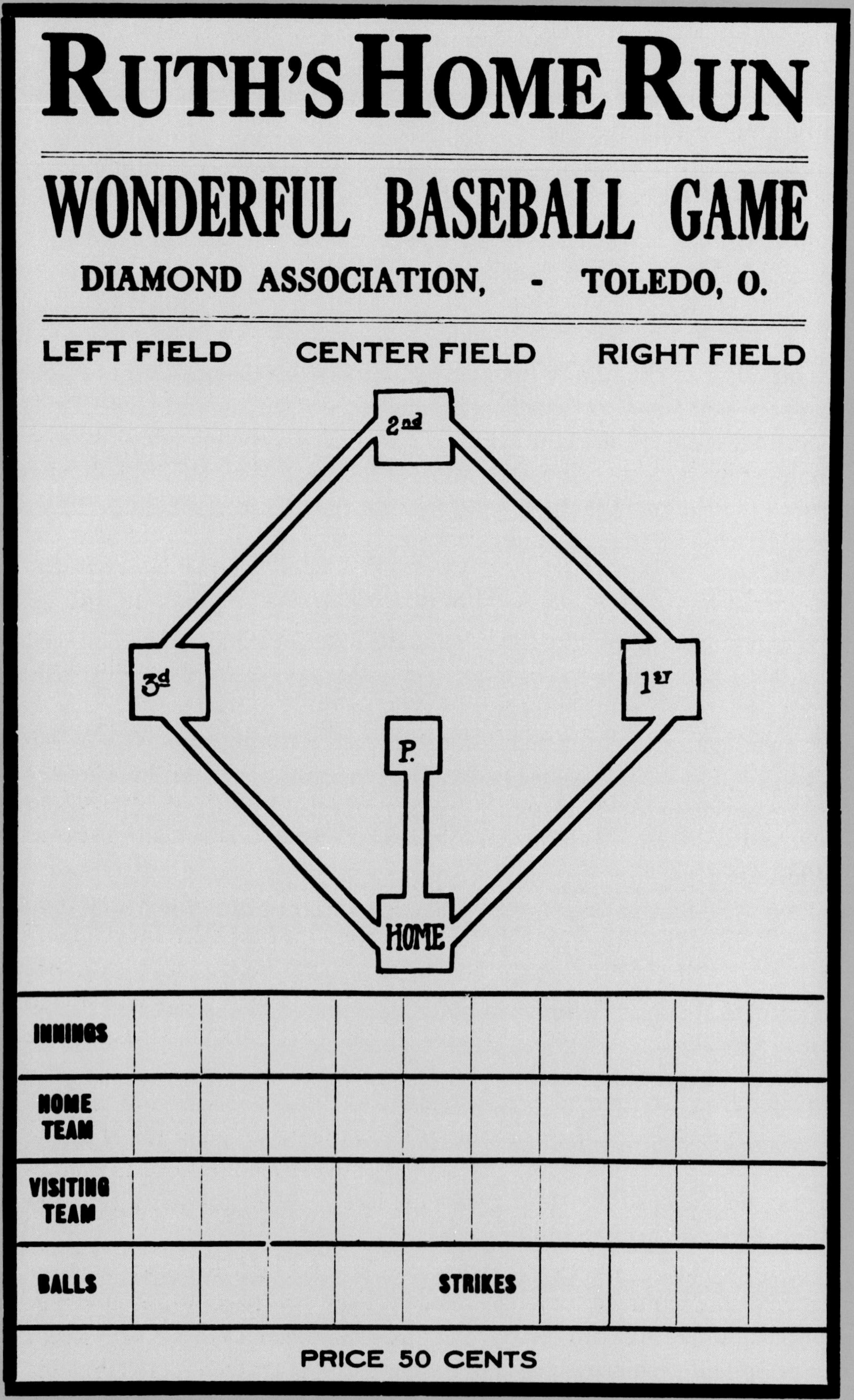
RUTH'S HOME RUN
WONDERFUL BASEBALL GAME
DIAMOND ASSOCIATION, - TOLEDO, O.
LEFT FIELD
CENTER FIELD
RIGHT FIELD
2nd
3d
1st
P.
HOME
INNINGS
HOME TEAM
VISITING TEAM
BALLS
STRIKES
PRICE 50 CENTS

suited him because 1920 turned out to be even better than 1919. He passed his single-season home run record of 29 in mid-July, but was going so fast it was only a blur. He ended with 54 home runs (25 more than his old record), 137 runs batted in, 158 runs scored, all league-leading figures, and a .376 batting average.

His slugging average (total bases divided by times at bat) was .847, which has never been even *approached* by anyone else. To put that .847 in perspective, Ted Williams's highest full-season slugging average was .735 (in 1941) and Mickey Mantle's was .705 (in 1956).

Babe Ruth's 54 home runs in 1920 were more than were hit by any other *team* in the American League other than the Yankees. Ruth hit 1 out of every 7 home runs hit in the league that year.

Hard as it is to believe, 1921 was again a better year: 59 home runs, once more a new record, 171 runs batted in, 177 runs scored, all league-leading, and a .378 batting average. His slugging percentage was down a notch—from .847 all the way down to .846.

It was during 1921 that he passed all existing lifetime home run records—both the post-1900 record of 119, held by Gavvy Cravath, and the pre-1900 record of 136, held by Roger Connor—and thereby, at age twenty-six, became the most prolific home run hitter of all time. Thereafter every home run he hit set a new record, a record that would eventually reach the sacrosanct number 714.

Late in the 1920 season it was discovered that eight of the Chicago White Sox—since known as the Black Sox—had been bribed by gamblers to throw the 1919 World Series to the Cincinnati Reds. Disillusioned fans wondered: if a World Series could be fixed, how many regular-season games were on the level?

That professional baseball survived, and even prospered, is due in good measure to Babe Ruth. His exploits overshadowed the shameful events of 1919 and soon eclipsed them. His tape-measure homers and magnetic personality so captured the imagination of the public that baseball soared in popularity and attendance reached unprecedented heights despite the scandal.

In fact, Ruth not only helped save baseball, he also remade it in his own image. Impressed by the enormous crowds he attracted, enthralled by the sweet music of the clicking turnstiles, the owners could read the handwriting on the cash register: if the fans liked home runs so much, then why not give 'em more of the same?

So in the early twenties the powers-that-be began to make changes designed to encourage long-ball hitting. They outlawed all pitches that involved tampering with or applying foreign substances to the ball except for the spitball, which could be thrown only by seventeen established big leaguers who were already using the pitch. The ball itself was also juiced up: a different kind of wool yarn was used and it was wound more tightly.

With pitchers restricted and the ball livelier, so-called inside baseball—bunting, the hit-and-run, place hitting—gave way to brawn and power, to swinging for the fences and double-digit scores. Only a few years out of a Baltimore reform school, and George Herman Ruth had already turned baseball upside down.

When they arrived in New York in 1920, the Babe and Helen moved into a suite at the Ansonia Hotel, on Broadway between Seventy-third and Seventy-fourth streets. As time passed, Helen stayed increasingly at their rural Sudbury home, near Boston, but Babe liked action and preferred the more exciting rhythm of the Ansonia. He bought a custom-built maroon Packard with a twelve-cylinder engine that his teammates called "the Ghost of Riverside Drive." Riverside Drive begins three blocks from the Ansonia, and the Babe dearly loved to drive his chariot along its sweeping curves in the early morning hours.

One reason Helen preferred Sudbury was because there was no privacy anywhere else. If they ate in a restaurant, went to a movie, took a walk—it didn't matter what they did or where they went—Ruth was mobbed. Youngsters dominated the crowds that surrounded him—he always seemed to have a special rapport with kids—but they were not alone. There was excitement whenever people spotted the familiar round face, the jaunty cap bobbing high above the ever-present sea of clamoring kids pulling and tugging at the sleeves of his tan camel's-hair coat.

Novelist James T. Farrell once described the sight of Babe Ruth after a game at Chicago's Comiskey Park in September of 1920: "As I was, myself, leaving the ball park, I saw Ruth. A crowd of over a hundred kids had him not only surrounded but almost mobbed. They pushed, shoved, scrambled and yelled so that Ruth could scarcely move. Wearing a blue suit, and a gray cap, there was an expression of bewilderment on his moon face. He said nothing, rolled with the kids and the strange, hysterical and noisy little mob slowly moved on to the exit gate with Ruth in the center of it. More kids rushed to the edge of the crowd and they, also, pushed and shoved, Ruth swayed from side to side, his shoulders bending one way, and then the other. As they all swirled to the gate, Ruth narrowly escaped being shoved into mustard which had been spilled from an overturned barrel. Ruth and the kids left the park, with the big fellow still in the center of the crowd of kids."

The Giants had always been top dog in New York until Ruth's arrival. Then, suddenly, the crowds at the Polo Grounds grew larger for the Yankees than for the Giants. The Yankees doubled their home attendance from 1919 to 1920; they drew almost 1,300,000 in 1920, the first team ever to break the million mark.

However, the Yankees were only tenants in the Polo Grounds, playing there at the dispensation of the Giants. Ruth's presence in the Yankee lineup jolted Giants Manager John McGraw. He had tried to get Ruth from Jack Dunn back in 1914 and was upset when Dunn sold him to the Red Sox. Since then it had been sour grapes.

"If he plays every day," McGraw had grumbled, when there was talk of the Red Sox switching Ruth to the outfield, "the big bum will hit into a hundred double plays a season."

Feeling they had worn out their welcome in the Polo Grounds, the Yankees built huge Yankee Stadium in the Bronx, right across the Harlem River from McGraw. Over 74,000 were reported in attendance and 25,000 more were turned away when the Stadium was festively inaugurated on April 18, 1923, Opening Day. As one would expect, the Babe christened it with a game-winning three-run homer into the right field bleachers—into Ruthville, as that section of the bleachers was soon called.

Sportswriter Fred Lieb, covering Opening Day for the *New York Evening Telegram,* referred to the magnificent new Stadium as "The House That Ruth Built"—which has been its name ever since.

Babe and Helen's country home and farm, 200 acres in Sudbury, Massachusetts, twenty miles west of Boston. Ruth liked to think of himself as a country squire, which only shows how little we understand ourselves; in reality he was a city boy through and through.

LEFT: George Herman Ruth in 1920 at the age of twenty-five.

As soon as he established his own home, the Babe wanted a puppy to go with it.
RIGHT: Golf became a passion with Ruth that almost rivaled baseball.

Edward Grant Barrow was, in Nelson Algren's words, "a hard guy." He managed the Red Sox from 1918 through 1920 and then switched over to the Yankees' executive suite, where he ran a tight ship for twenty-five years — first as general manager (the position was called "business manager" then) and subsequently as president.

BELOW: In 1894, at the age of twenty-six. At the time he was a clerk at the Staley Hotel in Pittsburgh.

Harry Frazee, owner of the Boston Red Sox from 1916 to 1923. The man who traded away Babe Ruth. It happened many years ago, but in Boston his reputation still rivals that of Judas Iscariot and Benedict Arnold.

LEFT: Pitcher Carl Mays. Traded from the Red Sox to the Yankees in 1919.

BELOW: Pitcher Waite Hoyt. Traded from the Red Sox to the Yankees in 1920.

RIGHT: Third baseman Joe Dugan. Traded from the Red Sox to the Yankees in 1922.

BELOW: Pitchers Herb Pennock and Babe Ruth. Pennock was traded from the Red Sox to the Yankees in 1923 — and Ruth, of course, in January of 1920.

The new boy in town. Babe Ruth joins the Yankees.

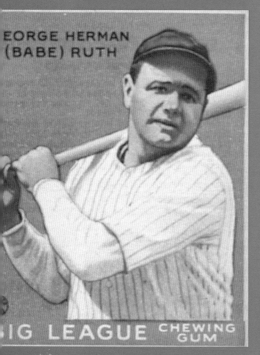

GEORGE HERMAN (BABE) RUTH

BIG LEAGUE CHEWING GUM

GEORGE HERMAN (BABE) RUTH

BIG LEAGUE CHEWING GUM

GEORGE HERMAN (BABE) RUTH

BIG LEAGUE CHEWING GUM

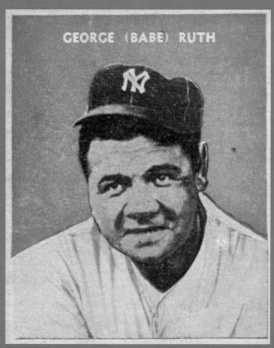

GEORGE (BABE) RUTH

BABE RUTH

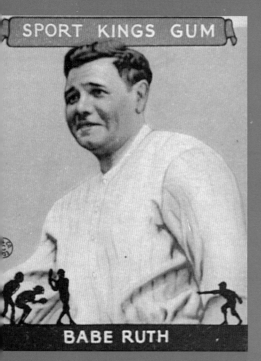

SPORT KINGS GUM

BABE RUTH

GEORGE HERMAN (BABE) RUTH

BIG LEAGUE CHEWING GUM

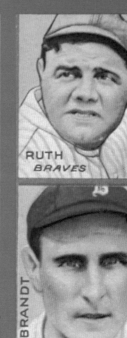

RUTH BRAVES

McMANUS BRAVES

BRANDT BRAVES

MARANVILLE BRAVES

LEFT: Baseball cards have generally increased in value and, not surprisingly, Babe Ruth cards typically command a premium price. All these cards were issued by gum or candy companies.

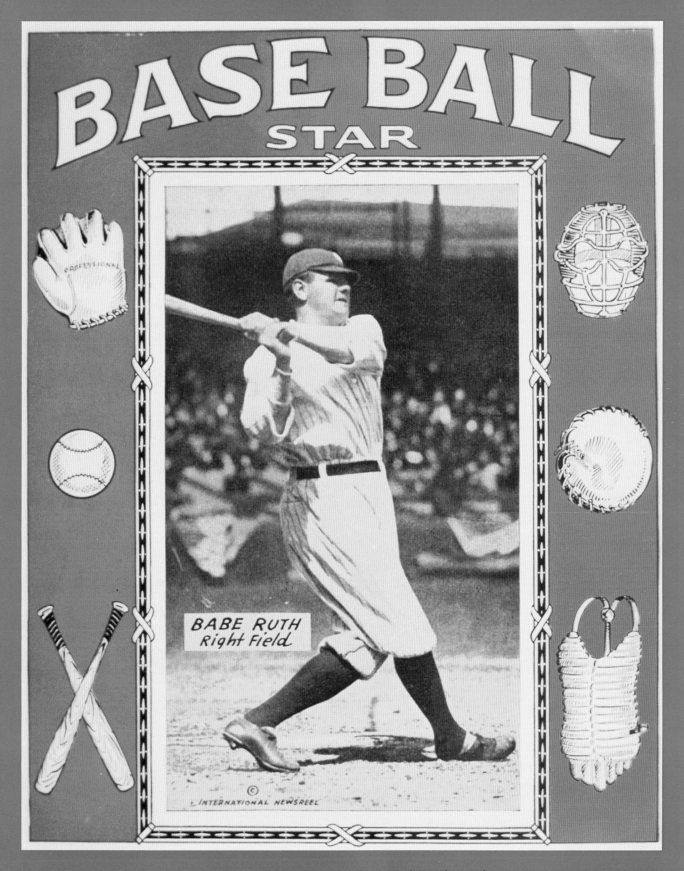

ABOVE: A schoolboy's notebook cover from the mid-1920s.

Some baseball memorabilia in the Babe Ruth Museum in Baltimore, Maryland, and in the collection of Barry Halper. The uniform is from Ruth's rookie year of 1914. The hat is probably 1920–21. The suitcase may be the very one that kept Ping Bodie company! And the ring is Ruth's 1927 World Series ring positioned within a charm bracelet.

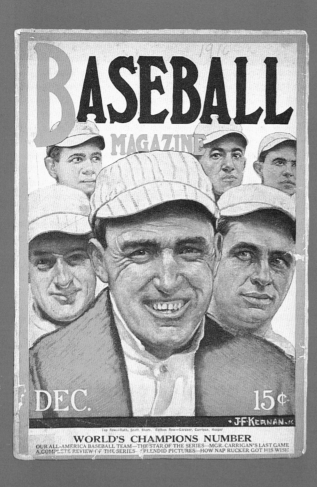

BASEBALL
MAGAZINE

DEC.   15¢

J.F.KERNAN.16

Top Row—Ruth, Scott, Shore. Bottom Row—Gardner, Carrigan, Hooper

WORLD'S CHAMPIONS NUMBER

OUR ALL-AMERICA BASEBALL TEAM—THE STAR OF THE SERIES—MGR. CARRIGAN'S LAST GAME
A COMPLETE REVIEW OF THE SERIES—SPLENDID PICTURES—HOW NAP RUCKER GOT HIS WISH

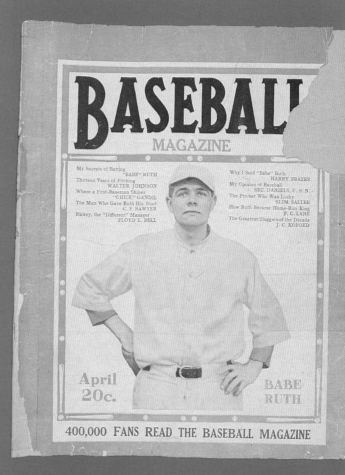

BASEBALL
MAGAZINE

My Secrets of Batting
"BABE" RUTH
Thirteen Years of Pitching
WALTER JOHNSON
Where a First-Baseman Shines
"CHICK" GANDIL
The Man Who Gave Ruth His Start
C. F. SAWYER
Rickey, the "Different" Manager
FLOYD L. BELL

Why I Sold "Babe" Ruth
HARRY FRAZEE
My Opinion of Baseball
SEC. DANIELS, U. S. N.
The Pitcher Who Was Lucky
SLIM SALLEE
How Ruth Became Home-Run King
F. C. LANE
The Greatest Sluggers of the Decade
J. C. KOFOED

April
20c.   BABE
                                          RUTH

400,000 FANS READ THE BASEBALL MAGAZINE

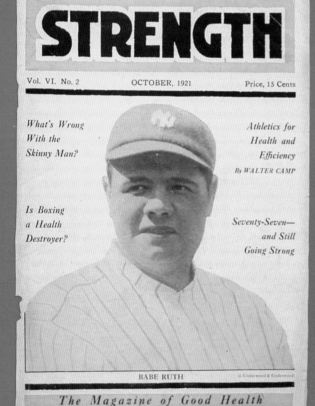

STRENGTH

Vol. VI. No. 2   OCTOBER, 1921   Price, 15 Cents

What's Wrong
With the
Skinny Man?

Is Boxing
a Health
Destroyer?

Athletics for
Health and
Efficiency
By WALTER CAMP

Seventy-Seven—
and Still
Going Strong

BABE RUTH   G. Underwood & Underwood

The Magazine of Good Health

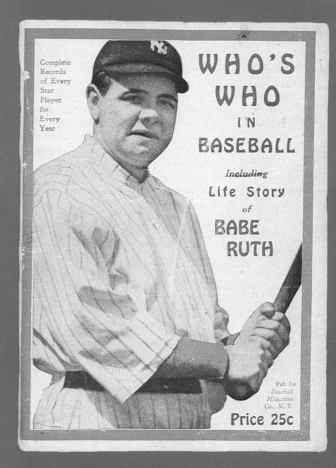

Complete
Records
of Every
Star
Player
for
Every
Year

WHO'S
WHO
IN
BASEBALL

Including

Life Story
of
BABE
RUTH

Pub by
Baseball
Magazine
Co., N. Y.

Price 25c

The
YOUTH'S COMPANION
combined with
American Boy
Founded 1827

April 1935

10¢

NRA CODE

"Good-by, Babe Ruth!"
by
H. G. SALSINGER

One Year $1

COVER PAINTING BY EDGAR FRANKLIN WITTMACK

Three Years $2

Babe Ruth was a magazine "cover boy" for twenty years . . . from 1916 to 1935.

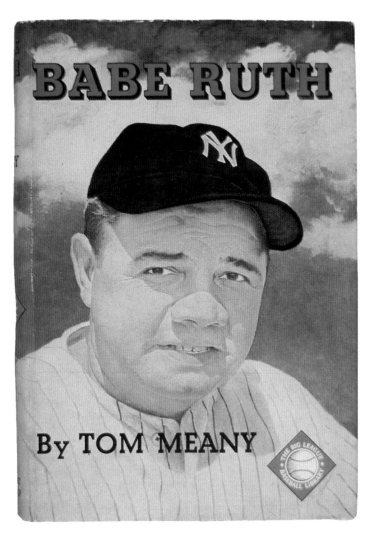

Two book covers—one book about the Babe and one by him.

Babe Ruth's personal Christmas card from 1931.
It is a combination photograph and water color.

For a generation, Ruth was the idol and inspiration
of virtually every American boy.

The Magic name and picture of Babe Ruth sold just about anything and everything— including, naturally, baseball games and baseball equipment.

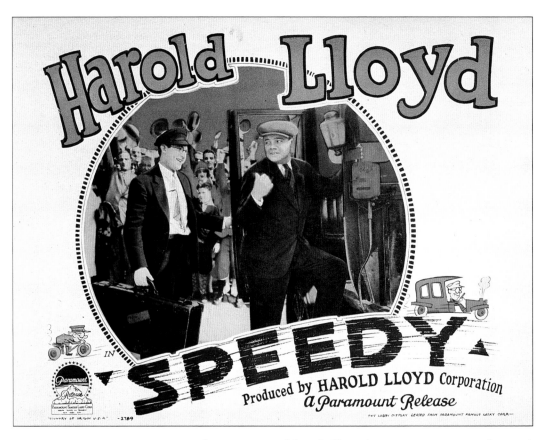

America's two great passions—the movies and baseball. *Babe Comes Home* and *Speedy* (in which Ruth had a cameo role) were both made in Hollywood in early 1927.

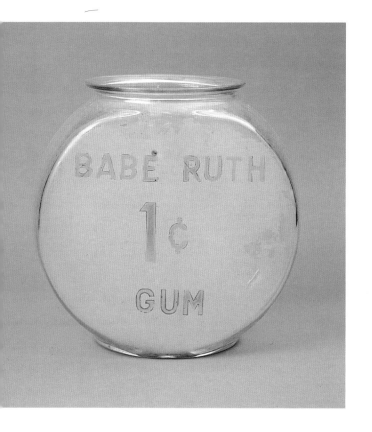

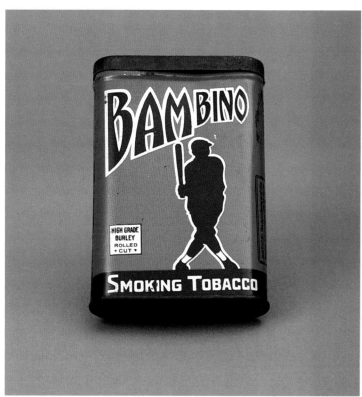

Christy Walsh was a busy man. It is hard to believe he could have missed many commercial opportunities. Babe's "Home Run" candy bar is long gone while "Baby Ruth" candy bars, from which he never made a penny, are as popular as ever.

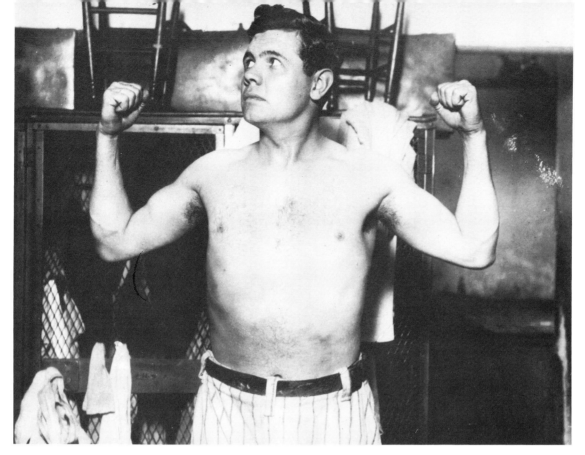

Ruth didn't always have the famous beer belly that later became his trademark.

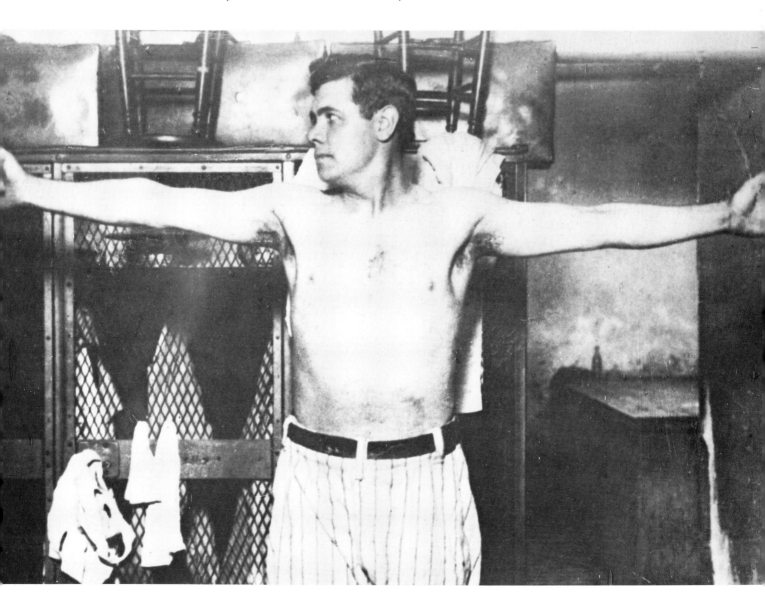

A young Ruth exploding out of the batter's box.

The ornate Beaux Arts exterior of the Ansonia apartment hotel, built in 1904 on Broadway between Seventy-third and Seventy-fourth streets. The Ruths lived here when they moved to New York in 1920. Other residents of the Ansonia have included tenor Enrico Caruso, conductor Arturo Toscanini, composer Igor Stravinsky, theatrical producer Flo Ziegfeld, and writer Theodore Dreiser.

Ruth has just parked his car and is walking toward the ballpark to get ready for a game. As usual, he has acquired an impromptu entourage, which he makes no attempt to discourage.

Helen was a frequent spectator at Yankee games when the Ruths first arrived in New York. Here she is at the Polo Grounds, then the home park of both the Yankees and Giants, in June of 1920.

Colonel Jacob Ruppert, in his mid-thirties, when he was serving four consecutive terms (1899 through 1906) as a Democratic congressman from New York City. Ruppert, a millionaire beer baron, bought the Yankees in 1915, along with Colonel T. L. Huston. In 1923 Ruppert bought out his partner and remained sole owner until his death sixteen years later.

Babe takes his manager, Miller Huggins, for a spin on Riverside Drive. Note his nifty gauntlet cuffs and the monogram on the car door.

Ruth demonstrating how to hit a baseball shot from one of those newfangled pitching machines.

Ruth and Yankee co-owner Colonel Tillinghast L'Hommedieu Huston. An engineer by profession, the colonel loved a good time as much as the Babe, so the two got along famously until Huston sold out to Ruppert in mid-1923 and departed from the scene.

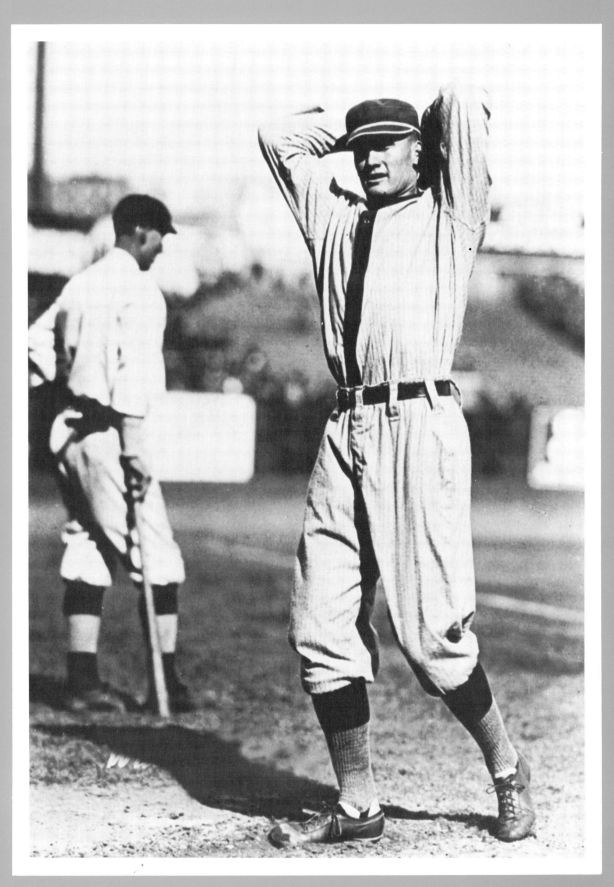

Walter Johnson. Although Walter was the greatest pitcher of his time — many say of all time — he did not fare well against Babe Ruth. They opposed each other as starting pitchers eight times from 1915 through 1918. Ruth won six games, Johnson two.

In home-town game, Babe comes to the plate and hits a homer that goes five blocks and smashes the new stained-glass window of the church.

1 Between ice deliveries, the Babe whittles on his homemade bat.

2 When her dog is taken to the pound, Babe gives his sister a lollypop.

3 Babe and sister sneak into the pound and let out all the stray dogs.

4 While taking ice to a church social, Babe stops off to play ball.

5 He gets to the social late and unhappy, the ice melting away.

In 1920 Babe Ruth made a long-forgotten silent movie called *Headin' Home.*

6 A home-loving young man, the Babe sups with mother and sister.

7 Lovelorn Babe wades out into a lake to greet his coy sweetheart.

8 When a pitcher gets drunk, the Babe takes his place.

9 The Babe's little sister helps him carry equipment to the game.

10 When sister brings his homemade bat, he wallops window-breaking homer.

11 Town spinster, defending Babe, shows swing to angry parishioners.

12 Minister saves Babe from being mobbed for breaking the window.

13 Babe stops his girl from eloping with his rival, then leaves town.

14 In the big city, Babe is a success on a major league team.

15 Babe persuades his girl's runaway brother to go back home.

16 Babe's home runs win the Series and he becomes a national hero.

17 Rich and famous, Babe comes back to his loving mother and sister.

Here are the story line and some scenes from the film.

President Warren G. Harding visits the ballpark. Politicians loved to be photographed shaking hands with the Babe, for obvious reasons. President Harding died unexpectedly in 1923; the cause of death has never been firmly established, because Mrs. Harding refused to permit an autopsy on her husband's body and, President or not, there was no law requiring it.

Manager John J. McGraw of the New York Giants and Babe Ruth size each other up prior to the 1922 World Series between the Giants and Yankees. Neither can quite manage a friendly smile. The two never did get along very well, dating from McGraw's reported comment, when the Babe was still a pitcher, that "if he plays every day the big bum will hit into a hundred double plays a season."

Ruth and Wally Schang in 1922. A hard-hitting catcher, Schang played on the Yankees for five years (1921–1925) and in the big leagues for nineteen (1913–1931).

At one time or another Babe endorsed just about everything, from anchovies to zippers. But one thing he never made a penny from was the Baby Ruth candy bar, which first appeared in 1921 and is still popular. The manufacturer insisted it wasn't named after Babe Ruth at all, but after the daughter of President Grover Cleveland — baby Ruth Cleveland. (In fact, baby Ruth Cleveland was born in 1891 and died of diphtheria in 1904, seventeen years before the candy bar's appearance.)

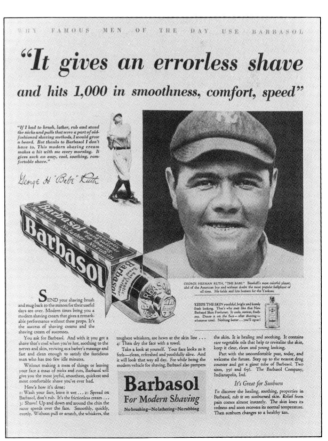

89

It is April 18, 1923, Opening Day for the spanking-new House That Ruth Built.

It is still April 18, and inside the bunting-draped ballpark Babe is posing with Yankee mascot Ray Kelly.

This shot of Ruth taking batting practice in the twenties shows how Yankee Stadium used to look, before the right field stands were extended into fair territory in 1937. The dimensions of the original Stadium were 295 feet down the right field line, 490 feet in straightaway center, and 281 feet down the left field line. (After the 1937 extension of the right field stands until the reconstruction that took place in 1974–1975, the comparable distances were 296 feet, 461 feet, and 301 feet.)

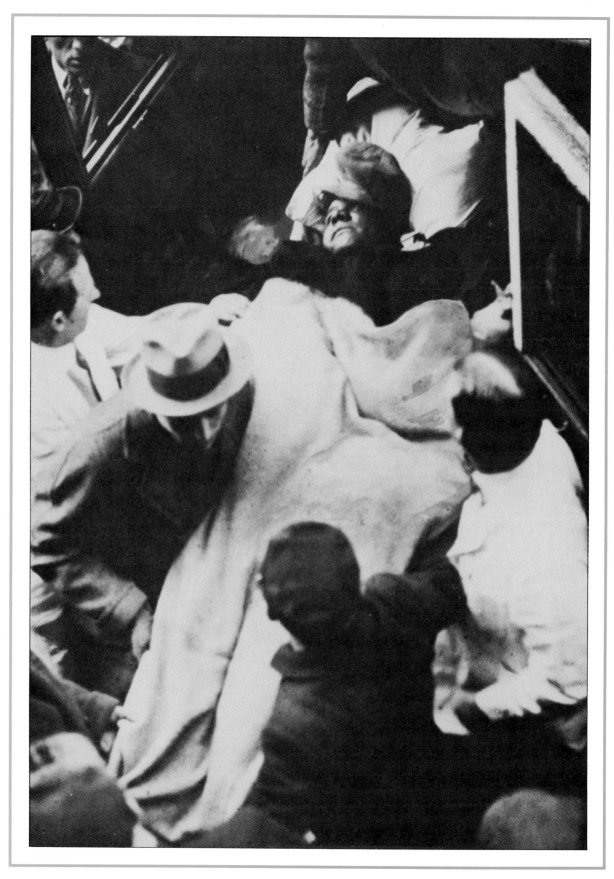

The bellyache heard round the world. It is shortly after 1 P.M. on April 9, 1925, and Babe Ruth is being lifted into an ambulance outside Pennsylvania Station so he can be rushed to St. Vincent's Hospital.

The Bellyache Heard Round the World

1922-1925

The Babe might have been at the pinnacle of the baseball universe, but his marriage was a mess. He wasn't home much, and even when he was, the family's privacy was invaded by a steady stream of visitors, many of them virtual strangers. Most of the time he was away somewhere while Helen lived by herself for lengthy periods in their home near Boston.

Perhaps to help relieve Helen's loneliness, in 1921 they adopted an infant daughter, whom they named Dorothy. In subsequent years Dorothy gave both of them much happiness, but her arrival failed to repair their deteriorating relationship. Although neither sought a divorce, largely because of religious beliefs, for all practical purposes the marriage was over by mid-1925.

But the rocky road of the Babe's private life was serenity itself compared to his public trials and tribulations. After the 1921 season, for example, Babe decided to pick up a few extra bucks playing postseason exhibition games. Commissioner Landis, however, issued an edict forbidding the tour. After the revelations of the Black Sox scandal, the widely respected Judge Kenesaw Mountain Landis had been appointed Commissioner of Baseball and given almost unlimited authority in an attempt to restore public confidence in baseball's integrity.

When told that Landis had turned thumbs down on his barnstorming tour, the Babe was annoyed: "Tell the old geezer he can go jump in a lake," he said (or words to that effect).

1922–1925   THE BABE

95

The judge's reaction was just as pungent: "Who does that big baboon think he is?" he fumed. "I'll show him who's running this show."

The barnstorming tour was a financial bust and, in addition, Ruth paid dearly for squaring off against the thin-skinned commissioner. The judge branded his behavior "mutinous defiance" and suspended him without pay until May 20, 1922, which meant for the first thirty-nine days of the approaching season.

When Ruth finally did get to play in 1922, he was out of shape and in a surly mood. On May 25, only five days after returning to the lineup, he singled to center and slid into second trying to stretch the single into a double. When umpire George Hildebrand called him out, he jumped up with a handful of dirt and furiously threw it in the umpire's face. Hildebrand promptly gave him the thumb, but instead of leaving the field Ruth jumped into the stands and angrily chased a loud-mouthed heckler up an aisle. Some police and Yankees dragged Ruth out of the stands, but before he departed for the clubhouse he stood on top of the Yankee dugout, like King Kong, and challenged all the fans in the ballpark.

"You're all yellow," he shouted, arms waving, face flushed.

He was let off remarkably lightly for such a temper tantrum—only a $200 fine and a one-day suspension—no doubt due to a certain amount of sympathy because he'd just completed a long period on the sidelines. (Also, he was the biggest drawing card in the game; without the Babe in the lineup, attendance would take a nose dive.)

A month later he got into similar trouble. On June 19 umpire Bill Dinneen made a disputed call at second base that went against the Yankees. As the argument raged in the infield, Ruth came running in from his position in left field determined to put in his two cents' worth. Apparently he said something the umpire took exception to, because Dinneen immediately ejected him from the game.

That night American League President Ban Johnson hit Babe with a three-day suspension for using "vulgar and vicious" language. It was lengthened to five days after Ruth cornered Dinneen during batting practice the following day and threatened the umpire with physical violence if Dinneen ever dared throw him out of a game again.

League President Johnson accompanied the suspension with a warning letter that read in part: "Your conduct was reprehensible . . . shocking to every American mother who permits her boy to go to a game. A man of your stamp bodes no good in the profession. The time has arrived when you should allow some intelligence to creep into a mind that has plainly been warped."

But the advice didn't take. On August 30 the Babe exploded again when umpire Tom Connolly called him out on strikes. He was thumbed out of the game and suspended for three days, once more for using "vulgar and vicious" language. When reporters tried to reach Ruth at the Ansonia, Helen said he was "out fishing." However, one source reported he spent at least part of his suspension in his old hometown, Baltimore, where he was said to have "barely escaped a police raid" on a speakeasy called Bowley's Quarters.

Ruth hit .315 in 1922, with 35 homers, 99 runs batted in, and 94 runs scored (with all his suspensions—five of them—he got in only 110 games). A pretty fair year for most players, but not a fitting one for the Babe.

If the season was bad, the World Series was worse. The Yankees lost to the Giants, four games to none (with one game a tie), and Ruth hit a measly .118. He got only two hits in all five games, a single and a double. Giants Manager John McGraw crowed that he "had the big monkey's number—just pitch him low curves and slow stuff and he falls all over himself."

In addition, Ruth was roundly booed in the third Series game when he barreled into little Heinie Groh, the popular Giant third baseman, and sent the 150-pounder sprawling. Groh was having a fine Series—he hit .474, which he proudly displayed on his automobile license plate for the rest of his life—and the collision looked deliberate.

At the end of the game, both Ruth and teammate Bob Meusel violated one of baseball's unwritten laws: they shoved their way into the Giants' locker room, looking for some players who had been heckling them. Fortunately, they were hustled back to their own clubhouse before any serious fisticuffs could develop.

If Babe Ruth wasn't the original Big Spender—easy come, easy go—he certainly was a reasonably good facsimile. The Babe's ability to squander money was as legendary as his prowess with the bat (or knife and fork). He saved absolutely nothing even though his $20,000 annual salary in 1920 was raised to $30,000 in 1921. At the start of the 1922 season he signed a five-year contract for $52,000 a year. The Yankees offered $50,000, but Ruth insisted on an additional $2,000 "because there are fifty-two weeks in a year and it would be nice to make a grand a week."

Oddly enough, perhaps to add a touch of humor, the contract contained a morals clause which stipulated that Ruth must "refrain and abstain entirely from the use of intoxicating liquors and shall not stay up later than one a.m. without the permission and consent of the club's manager." There is no evidence that the Yankees ever took the clause seriously, and twenty-seven-year-old George H. Ruth surely didn't.

Fifty-two thousand a year, a quarter million over five years, was an absolutely enormous amount of money in the twenties. It is *still* a lot of money, despite the fact that taxes and prices have soared since then. Even so, aside from his Yankee salary Ruth was realizing only a small fraction of his potential earning power: his name was magic but he was not capitalizing on it.

At about that time, fortunately for Ruth, a resourceful and imaginative young man named Christy Walsh managed to slip into Ruth's suite at the Ansonia on the pretense of delivering a case of bootleg beer from the neighborhood delicatessen. Walsh grew up in California, where he graduated from St. Vincent's College in Los Angeles in 1911. He passed the state bar examination several years later and was licensed to practice law there, but moved to New York because he was more interested in the business aspects of the sports and entertainment industries.

"Mr. Ruth, how much do you get for those newspaper articles you write?" Walsh asked, after stowing away the beer in the kitchen. (Ruth, or rather a sportswriter on his behalf, authored a brief story for a local paper, usually only a paragraph or so in length, after each home run that he hit.)

"Oh, five dollars, I think," Ruth answered, hardly looking up from what he was doing. "And why is it any of your business, anyway?"

"Mr. Ruth, I can get you hundreds of dollars for each article. And in addition I can guarantee you a *thousand* dollars within sixty days from similar deals."

That woke Ruth up. After serious discussion, they came to an agreement, and from then on, all Ruth's commercial ventures were cleared through and administered by Christy Walsh. For the rest of Ruth's career, Walsh served as his business representative and financial adviser. Under Walsh's guidance, he made perhaps twice as much annually from endorsements, exhibition games, and barnstorming tours as he made from his celebrated Yankee contracts. (The rules regarding barnstorming were eased in 1922.) And because of Walsh's insistence that he invest a portion of his earnings in annuities, to provide income in later years, Ruth became a wealthy man in retirement despite his spendthrift instincts.

Ruth did indeed receive a check for a thousand dollars from Walsh within, not sixty, but *thirty* days of their initial talk, which reassured Babe that he'd done the right thing. (What Ruth didn't know was that his clever agent had borrowed the money in order to get started on the right track with his valuable new client.)

On November 15, 1922, after his depressing suspension-riddled season, Babe attended a baseball writers' dinner at the New York Elks Club that would have a significant bearing on his career. After dinner, one speaker after another criticized the Babe's recent behavior. Near midnight, the featured speaker, New York State Senator James J. Walker (later Mayor

Jimmy Walker) rose to address the group. A spellbinder, he startled the audience with his first words: "Babe Ruth is not only a great athlete; he is also a great fool!"

He went on to discuss Ruth's excessive drinking, his temper tantrums, his late hours, his failure to stay in shape. "Worst of all," he continued, "you have let down the kids of America. They look up to you, worship you. And then what happens? It is exactly as though Santa Claus himself suddenly were to take off his beard to reveal the features of a villain. The kids have seen their idol shattered and their dreams broken."

At first Ruth's face showed anger and resentment. But then he began to sob. "If we didn't love you, Babe, I wouldn't say these things." More sobs from Ruth. Walker paused a long time and then finally broke the silence: "Babe, are you going to once again let down those dirty-faced kids in the streets of America?" he asked.

Through his tears, Ruth swore he'd mend his ways: "So help me, Jim, I'll go to the country and get in shape," he blubbered.

Of course, Jimmy Walker was hardly the one to give a Boy Scout lecture to anyone. Handsome and debonair, an aficionado of the well-turned female ankle, he was elected mayor of New York in 1925 and then reelected in 1929. But when corruption charges were leveled against him and his administration, he hastily resigned in 1932 and fled the country. On the eve of World War II, he was allowed to return to the United States, where he lived quietly in New York until his death in 1946.

The Babe kept his word. He did indeed "go to the country and get in shape." He spent most of the winter of 1922–1923 with Helen and little Dorothy at their country home outside of Boston, chopping wood and laying off the booze. By Opening Day 1923, when he christened the House That Ruth Built with his game-winning homer, his weight was down to 215 pounds, a good 20 pounds less than it had been, and his body was firm and trim.

As a matter of fact, he stayed that way—well, more or less—for the next two years. In 1923 he led the American League with 41 home runs and 131 runs batted in and hit .393, the highest batting average of his career. He also received 170 bases on balls, which is still a record, and even stole 17 bases just for good measure. There have always been arguments about which year was Ruth's best: 1920, 1921, or 1927. But Babe himself always said none of the above—his choice was 1923.

The Yankees won their third straight pennant in 1923 and, for the first time, trounced John McGraw's New York Giants in the World Series, four games to two. Something went awry with McGraw's formula for getting Ruth out, because the Babe hit three homers in the Series, as well as a triple, a double, and two singles, and batted a healthy .368.

Jimmy Walker's wandering boy had made it all the way back and then

Babe Ruth becomes a lieutenant in the New York Police Reserve. He objected to being fingerprinted when inducted. "I thought that was for the robbers," he said, "not the cops."

some. However, the Babe was never one to let success interfere with a good time, and as the 1924 season commenced he once again began to seek out his old haunts, return to his old ways.

And why not? Wasn't he Babe Ruth—the Behemoth of Bust, the Colossus of Clout, the Caliph of Clout, the Maharajah of Mash, the Rajah of Rap, the Sultan of Swat, the Wazir of Wham! The sportswriters loved him. The headline writers loved him even more; aside from "Babe," their favorite name for Ruth was "Bambino," which is Italian for "Babe" and was often shortened to simply "Bam."

"BAM HITS ONE" was a common headline of the day.

No ill effects of his carousing during the 1924 season were immediately apparent. He led the league in batting average, with .378, as well as in home runs (46), and runs scored (143), although his 121 runs batted in trailed Goose Goslin's 129. For the third year in four he had 200 or more base hits and for the fifth year in six over 100 runs batted in.

But 1925 would be another story altogether.

Not-so-young Babe Ruth, thirty years old on February 6, 1925, knew he had problems as he looked ahead to his twelfth year in the big leagues. He'd been on a six-month eating/drinking binge and it showed: on his birthday, he tipped the scales at a hefty 255 pounds, a good 35 or 40 pounds over his optimum playing weight of 215 to 220. Of course, his playing weight had once been in the 195-to-200-pound range, but that was long ago.

In 1924 and 1925 Ruth began to nurture the beer belly that eventually became his trademark. Until then he had generally been in relatively good shape; in the early twenties, of course, he did acquire a comfortable small paunch, but it was nothing special, just a little baby pillow. By 1925, though, the Babe Ruth profile familiar to later generations began to emerge: the big overhanging bay window atop skinny legs tapering down to spindly ankles. (The disproportion created an optical illusion that made his legs and ankles look thinner and weaker than they really were.)

Thereafter it was a never-ending battle, with newspapers reporting every spring on the Babe's determination to get in shape and his agonizing struggle to sweat off excess poundage.

In February of 1925, however, he seemed confused, unable to decide what he wanted: less weight or more. He went to Hot Springs, Arkansas, where he took the steam baths and exercised in order to slim down prior to joining the team in Florida. But if he lost five pounds in the daytime he'd put them right back on at night. His appetite was huge—for food, for whiskey, and for women. He couldn't get enough of any or all of them. He caught the flu before leaving Hot Springs for St. Petersburg, and when he arrived in Florida, Miller Huggins became concerned: "Babe, you look sick," he said.

The Yankees and Dodgers left Florida late in March of 1925 and played daily exhibition games as they traveled north by train toward New York for Opening Day on Tuesday, April 14. In Atlanta, Ruth felt ill—chills and fever—but insisted on accompanying the team to the next stop, Chattanooga, where he felt too sick for batting practice but thrilled the crowd with two home runs once the game began. He hit still another the next day in Knoxville. He was sick again that night, with stomach cramps and fever, but stayed with the team instead of going directly home to New York and a physician's care. He was batting .449 for the spring's exhibition games, highest on the club.

The teams left Knoxville early in the morning for Asheville, North Carolina, a winding and bumpy train ride through the Great Smoky Mountains that made several of the players nauseous. Ruth was miserable, not only nauseous but also burning up with fever. When the train finally arrived in Asheville, Ruth got off and promptly fainted. If catcher Steve O'Neill hadn't caught him, Ruth would probably have hit his head on the station's marble floor and fractured his skull.

Babe was sent on to New York by train, accompanied by Yankee scout Paul Krichell. As their train approached Penn Station, Krichell helped Ruth to the washroom and left him by himself. Alone, Ruth fell again, hit his head against the washbasin, and knocked himself out. Krichell got him back to his berth and revived him, but before the train entered the station Ruth collapsed again.

He was taken by stretcher from the train to an ambulance that rushed him to St. Vincent's Hospital on West Eleventh Street, where several days later he was operated on for an "intestinal abscess." His recovery was slow: he was in St. Vincent's almost seven weeks, from April 9 through May 25. He didn't play his first game of the 1925 season until June 1.

What was wrong with the Babe? "The bellyache heard round the world," wrote sportswriter W. O. McGeehan of the *New York Tribune*, and so it is often described to this very day. Tradition has it that Ruth ate so many hot dogs and drank so much soda pop on the train ride from Knoxville to Asheville that he had an attack of acute indigestion.

But that's a fairy tale. It was indeed in character for Babe to stuff himself with hot dogs and soda pop, but on this particular occasion he simply didn't. He was sick before he ever boarded the train to Asheville, had been sick on and off for weeks. The doctors used terms as "influenza," "indigestion," and "intestinal abscess," and said little more.

On the other hand, many newspapermen and teammates strongly suspected it was a venereal disease: either gonorrhea, syphilis, or both. Ed

Barrow, Ruth's manager in Boston, the man who had switched him from the mound to the outfield, thought it was syphilis and said so off the record. Barrow had come to New York from the Boston Red Sox in 1921 to become general manager of the Yankees, a position he held for a quarter of a century. Presumably Barrow, as a top Yankee official, got his information from the doctors.

Regardless of the facts—and no one any longer really knows what they were—the illness will always be known in folklore as "the bellyache heard round the world": a bellyache that required surgery and a seven-week hospital stay!

Dorothy, born in 1921, was adopted as an infant by Helen and Babe.

Judge Kenesaw Mountain Landis, Commisioner of Baseball from November 1920 until his death in 1944. Previously he had been a federal judge for the Northern District of Illinois. In 1921 he and George Herman Ruth squared off over the issue of postseason barnstorming and it was the judge who emerged victorious. Ruth and teammate Bob Meusel were suspended without pay for the first six weeks of the 1922 season.

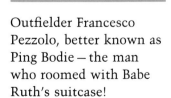

Outfielder Francesco Pezzolo, better known as Ping Bodie — the man who roomed with Babe Ruth's suitcase!

It is April 20, 1922, Opening Day, and the flag is being raised at the Polo Grounds. Under suspension, Ruth watches in civilian clothes.

It is still April 20, 1922. Uncharacteristically glum, Ruth sees the Yankees whip the Washington Senators, 10–3.

Colonel Jacob Ruppert with his two wayward ballplayers, Babe Ruth and Bob Meusel. It was about the taciturn and often grumpy Meusel that sportswriter Frank Graham once said, near the end of the outfielder's career, "He's learning to say hello when it's time to say good-bye."

It is May 20, 1922, and umpires Brick Owens (facing camera) and Oliver Chill are duly informing Ruth and Meusel that their suspensions are hereby lifted. Manager Lee Fohl of the opposing St. Louis Browns is an engrossed observer. (Note the megaphone, used in those days to announce pitchers and catchers.)

In the early twenties Christy Walsh began to put the Babe's chaotic financial affairs in some kind of order. One of Walsh's favorite income-generating schemes was to hire "ghost-writers" to put Ruth's thoughts on paper, with the articles signed by Ruth. Here the Babe tells one of his ghosts what to write!

Sportswriter Bill Slocum was the Babe's favorite alter ego: "You know," he once confided to Walsh, "I think Bill writes more like I do than anyone I know."

Sometimes the Babe simply took matters into his own hands.

Child actor Jackie Coogan — star of *The Kid* (1920) and *Peck's Bad Boy* (1921) — meets the Babe as Colonel Ruppert beams.

Left to right: George Herman Ruth, Edward Grant Barrow, and Yankee co-owner Tillinghast L'Hommedieu Huston.

The baseball writers' dinner at the Elks Club in New York on November 15, 1922, at which James J. Walker, then a rising young state senator, posed his dramatic question: "Babe, are you going to once again let down those dirty-faced kids in the streets of America?"

"So help me, Jim, I'll go to the country and get in shape," Ruth blubbered through his tears.

The papier-mâché cow on which Ruth is leaning was supposed to symbolize the "Back to the Farm" theme that Christy Walsh and Jimmy Walker had devised for the occasion.

The Babe was true to his word. He did indeed spend most of the winter of 1922–1923 with Helen and little Dorothy at the farm in Massachusetts. Over the winter he successfully shed twenty pounds.

Ruth and Jimmy Walker (both kneeling on the grass), after the debonair Walker
had become mayor of New York. He was forced to resign hastily in 1932 amid
charges of graft and corruption.

The date is October 10, 1923, and it is the first game of the World Series, Yankees vs. Giants. Ruth is sliding into third base for a fifth-inning triple. The third baseman is Heinie Groh, the umpire Eugene Hart, and the third base coach probably Charlie O'Leary.

Now it is October 11, the fifth inning of the second game of the '23 Series. A happy Babe Ruth is being escorted back to the dugout by Yankee batboy Eddie Bennett after hitting his second home run of the game.

Babe usually dressed impeccably, both
on and off the field.

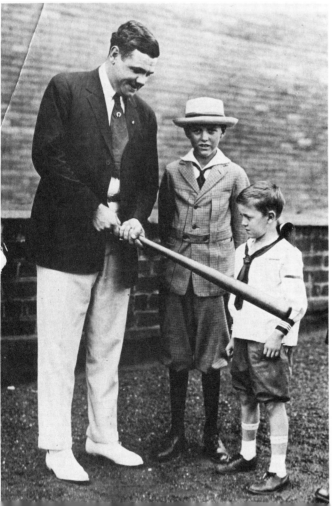

But not always.

The Ruth family in
the mid-twenties.

117

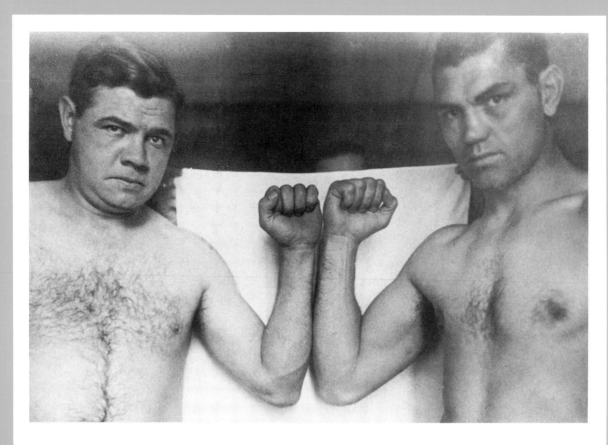

Two heavy hitters: Babe Ruth and Jack Dempsey, heavyweight boxing champion of the world from 1919 to 1926.

In 1925 twenty-two-year-old Lou Gehrig became a Yankee regular, thereby creating the most potent one-two punch in the history of the game. Ruth typically batted third and Gehrig fourth, which is why they were given 3 and 4, respectively, when numbers were introduced by the Yankees in 1929.

Ruth and Gehrig were inseparable for years, although there was a five-year break in their friendship starting in 1934. Here they are "bone-rubbing" their bats in order to preserve and harden the wood.

BABE
RUTH
Home Run
Champion

BABE RUTH
P.—Boston Red Sox
151

① "BABE" RUTH
King of them all.
Home Run Candy Bar.
His Candy Helped Him.

② "BABE" RUTH
Knocked out 60 Home
Runs in 1927.
His Candy Helped Him.

BABE RUTH

"Babe" Ruth
C.F. Yankees

"BABE" RUTH
P.—Boston Red Sox
147

Look Out, Mr. Pitcher!
This is the formidable picture the enemy slabman has to face. All of the "Babe's" bats have names. He made his 1926 record with "Black Betsy," a brunette, afterwards broken. The one in the picture is the King's current favorite, "Big Bertha," an ash blond.

Geo. H. "Babe" Ruth
OUTFIELDER, NEW YORK, AM. L.

Ruth is a Crack Fielder
The Big Leagues cannot boast a surer fielder than the Home Run King. The photograph shows him scooping up a liner preparatory to a double play that retired the opposing team and put the game on ice for the World's Champions.

Babe Ruth

BABE RUTH

"Babe" Ruth
"YANKEES"

YOUR OLD FRIEND
AND THE KIDS OUT TO S
BABE RUTH

Postseason barnstorming became a regular part of Ruth's life and the source of a substantial portion of his annual income from the mid-twenties to the mid-thirties. At left, he's in Scranton, Pennsylvania. The local dignitary is Sheriff Jim Reap.

ABOVE: In Sharon, Pennsylvania.

RIGHT: Today's game is in Iron Mountain, Michigan, and the local hero is Nello "Fungo" Tedeski.

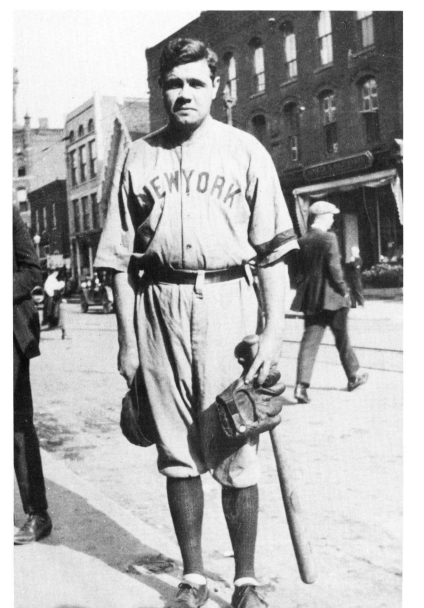

The barnstormers usually started on the East Coast and gradually wended their way west. Here they are in Nicollet Park in Minneapolis, and the Babe has decided to become a first baseman. Actually, he did play first base once in a while in the big leagues.

Barnstorming players often changed into their uniforms in the hotel and then walked to the ballpark.

While barnstorming, Ruth frequently visited hospitals and orphanages. Here he's at St. Ann's Home in Tacoma, Washington. Sportswriter Tom Meany said that "every public appearance Ruth made, in his playing days or thereafter, was an inconvenience and an annoyance. But Babe never once turned down a promise to go somewhere and visit some kids unless it was because he had a previous obligation to visit kids somewhere else."

LEFT: At Dunsmuir, California. BELOW: Players from Mount Shasta and Dunsmuir pose with Ruth's barnstorming team. Bob Meusel, on Ruth's right, is the only other major league ballplayer in the group. Fifty years later the others were still telling their grandchildren about the day they played with Babe Ruth.

Little Dorothy is not so little anymore.

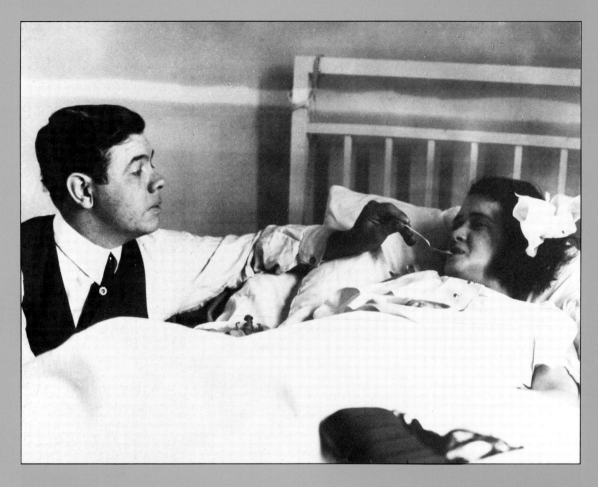

128

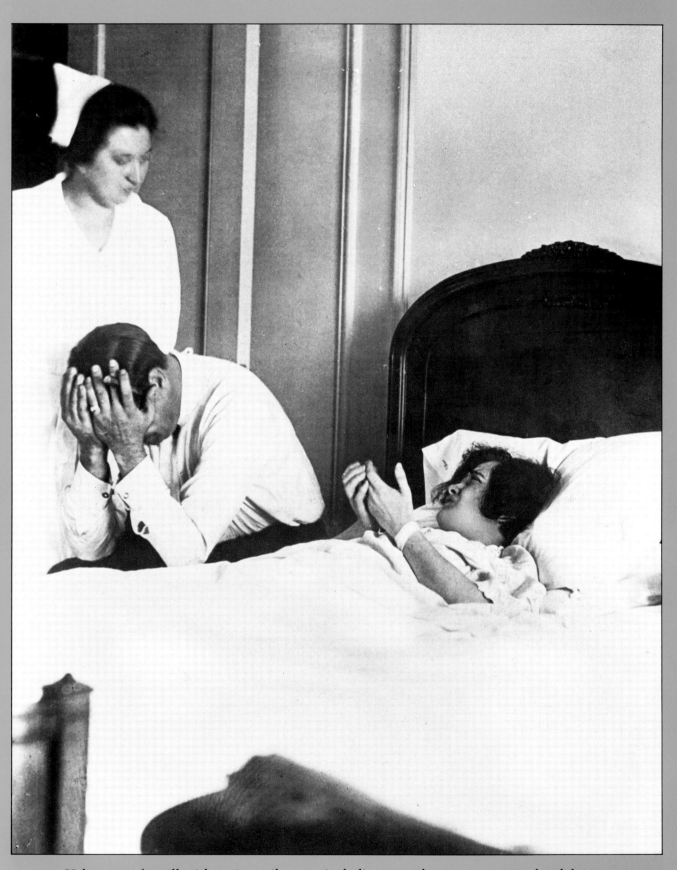

Helen was often ill with various ailments, including several apparent nervous breakdowns.

The Babe thoroughly enjoyed a good time, and it didn't much matter whether the setting was rural or urban.

With Dorothy at St. Vincent's on May 7. He has been in the hospital a month and won't leave for close to three more weeks. He won't play his first game of the 1925 season until June 1. Not coincidentally, the Yankees ended next to last in the American League in 1925, 28½ games behind the pennant-winning Washington Senators.

The Sultan of Swat

1925-1928

Memories of pain can be mercifully short. After returning to action on June 1, 1925, Ruth wasted little time in resuming the very life-style that had just landed him in St. Vincent's Hospital. The New York Yankees were a demoralized team that year. After winning the pennant in 1921, '22, and '23, and finishing a close second in 1924, they went into a tailspin and fell to seventh in 1925. Since they won again in 1926, '27, and '28, their 1925 nose dive must be attributed in large part to Ruth's "bellyache" and his subsequent erratic behavior.

Babe never did think much of little Manager Miller Huggins to begin with, and he blatantly refused to follow the rules Huggins laid down. It wasn't that Ruth didn't like short men. His best friends on the Yankees included outfielder Whitey Witt and catcher Benny Bengough, both of whom were about the same size as Huggins.

Indeed, it was reportedly Benny Bengough who gave Ruth the name by which he was known to his Yankee teammates: "Jidge" (or "Jidgie"), pronounced like "judge" except for an "id" sound in place of the "ud." No one is sure of its origin, but it was generally assumed to be a corruption of "George."

"Jidge" wasn't used when talking *about* Ruth, only when talking *to* him. In talking about him, players usually referred to him as "the Babe" or more often "the big fellow" or "the big guy." Sportswriter Tom Meany once commented that "if you mentioned 'the big fellow' to anybody in the American League over the twenty-year period when Ruth was hitting home runs, he'd have known instantly whom you meant."

The basic problem was that Ruth never did like *anyone* telling him what to do: his parents put him in reform school because he was uncontrollable; he almost came to blows with Ed Barrow, his manager at Boston; he got suspended for defying Landis's edict against barnstorming; and he was continually battling against the rulings of umpires. Huggins was just another in a long line of authority figures challenged by the Babe.

When he returned to the lineup on June 1, 1925, Ruth acted as though St. Vincent's had been a vacation resort, a way station provided for his convenience in preparing further assaults on the citadels of wine, women, and song. This time, however, he was vulnerable. His home run production was puny and even singles were hard to come by; in August he was still batting below .250. League-leading home run hitters can get away with a lot more than thirty-year-olds struggling to hit their weight.

Huggins warned him several times to cut out his after-hours rambling, to get back to the hotel by the 1 A.M. curfew. Ruth shrugged. With the team going nowhere, his players out of control, Huggins finally decided to take a stand. He asked for and received approval from Colonel Ruppert and Ed Barrow to take whatever disciplinary measures he thought appropriate.

On a western swing in late August, Ruth stayed out all night two nights in a row in St. Louis, always one of his favorite towns. On the afternoon of August 29, still in St. Louis, he breezed into the Yankee locker room right before game time, too late to take batting practice.

"Hi," he said casually to Huggins, "had some personal business to take care of."

"You've had too much personal business to take care of lately," snapped Huggins. "Don't bother to suit up. You're suspended and you're fined $5,000. Now get out of here and take the next train back to New York."

After an angry explosion and a tirade of abuse against Huggins, Ruth stormed out of the locker room. He was in no mood, however, to meekly obey the manager's order and take the next train home. Instead he sought comfort and solace in familiar surroundings, namely, at the House of the Good Shepherd, widely known as the city's most opulent brothel.

"I'm through with the Yankees," he told anyone who would listen. "I'll never play for Huggins again. Either he goes or I do."

He arrived in New York several days later and went to Ruppert's office trailed by a small army of reporters. But the colonel backed Huggins, not Ruth: "The fine and the suspension stand," said Ruppert. "When Ruth apologizes to Huggins, the manager will decide when to reinstate him."

A chastened, subdued, and more realistic Babe Ruth was finally allowed back in the lineup on September 7, after an appropriate apology had been offered and accepted. But the $5,000 fine was not rescinded. It was almost 10 percent of Ruth's annual salary; a comparable fine imposed on one of today's $2-million-a-year ballplayers would amount to $200,000. (Ruppert eventually did return the money, but only after the death of Huggins four years later.)

In terms of numbers, 1925 was the Babe's worst year. He played in fewer than a hundred games, had only 25 home runs, just 66 runs batted in, and a .290 batting average. The general impression around the league was that he was through.

He'd be thirty-one the next year, in February of 1926. At that age, most ballplayers of the day were starting to wonder how they'd pay the rent, much less keep on living in style, as the big paychecks dwindled down to a precious few. Especially ballplayers who never learned how to take care of themselves. Ballplayers like Babe Ruth, for instance.

That winter, at the annual New York Baseball Writers' Dinner, sportswriter Rud Rennie, in the role of Miller Huggins, sang a parody written by Bill Slocum:

> I wonder where my Babe Ruth is tonight?
> He grabbed his hat and coat and ducked from sight.
>   I wonder where he'll be
>   At half past two or three?
> He may be at a dance or in a fight.
> He may be at some cozy roadside inn.
> He may be drinking tea—or maybe gin.
>   I know he's with a dame,
>   I wonder what's her name?
> I wonder where my Babe Ruth is tonight?

At the end of the 1925 season, it was almost universally believed that Ruth was a has-been—that was the consensus in the dugouts, in the press boxes, in the grandstands and the bleachers. Whether he ate, drank, or screwed himself out of baseball was the only question at issue.

As it turned out, however, all he had been doing in his first six years with the Yankees, from 1920 through 1925, was getting ready for the main event. Because in the following six years, from 1926 through 1931, he went on what can only be described as a batting rampage that has never been equaled before or since. His home run figures for that six-year period were 47, 60, 54, 46, 49, and 46. He led the league in homers every single year. His runs batted in were 145, 164, 142, 154, 153, and 163. He led the league in RBIs twice, in runs scored three times, in bases on balls five times, and in slugging percentage six times. His year-by-year batting averages were .372, .356, .323, .345, .359, and .373. And just to show he could still do it, he *pitched* the last game of the 1930 season, went the full nine innings, and won by a score of 9–3.

In Robert Creamer's words, from 1926 through 1931, Ruth "put on the finest display of hitting that baseball has ever seen. He hit his 300th home run the day after Huggins reinstated him, but there were more than 400 yet to come. He had been a dominant figure in six World Series, but the best of his World Series were still ahead of him. From the ashes of 1925, Babe Ruth rose like a rocket."

In December of 1925 a grim-faced Babe Ruth started working out in Artie McGovern's gymnasium at Forty-second Street and Madison Avenue. His weight was 254 flabby pounds. McGovern put him on a rigorous program of exercise, diet, and rest. Ruth didn't try to kid himself or anyone else. He took the training regimen seriously and worked at it diligently—so diligently, in fact, that two months later, when he reported to St. Petersburg for spring training, he weighed a solid 212. A beaming Artie McGovern said he was in tip-top shape. Apparently, George Herman Ruth was finally starting to learn some self-discipline.

The Yankees started fast in 1926 and kept up the pace all season. It was Lou Gehrig's first full year as Yankee first baseman: the twenty-three-old former Columbia University student hit .313 and led the league in triples. The New Yorkers won the pennant in a tremendous comeback after their dismal seventh-place finish in 1925.

However, they lost the World Series in seven games to the St. Louis Cardinals, despite the heroics of both Gehrig and Ruth. Gehrig batted .348 in the Series, while Ruth hit .300 and had 4 home runs, 3 of them in the fourth game. This was the first time anyone had hit 3 home runs in one World Series game.

The 1926 World Series has become famous because of the seventh inning of the seventh game, when thirty-nine-year-old Grover Cleveland Alexander came in from the bullpen to strike out Yankee rookie Tony Lazzeri with the bases loaded, thereby saving the victory for St. Louis. It was the last Series the Yankees would lose until 1942, when St. Louis would beat them again. In between, though, New York won the World Series in 1927, '28, '32, '36, '37, '38, '39, and '41.

The 1927 Yankees—still believed by many to be the greatest baseball team of all time—won the pennant by nineteen games over second-place Philadelphia and then took four straight from Pittsburgh in the World Series. During the regular season Gehrig hit 47 homers and Ruth 60, with

Ruth thereby breaking his own single-season home run record (59, set in 1921). There was tremendous excitement when the Babe hit his 60th off Tom Zachary of the Washington Senators on September 30, although some blasé fans refused to join in the celebration—they figured he'd probably break his own record again next year, so what was the big deal!

The following year, 1928, was essentially a repeat of 1927. The Yankees won the pennant and then took four straight from the Cardinals in the World Series. During the regular season Gehrig hit 27 homers, Ruth 54. In the Series, Gehrig hit .545 with four home runs, while Ruth batted .625 with three home runs, all in the fourth game. This was the second time anyone had hit three home runs in one World Series game; it wouldn't be done again until 1977 (by Reggie Jackson).

Babe Ruth was riding the crest. He was performing at the peak of his ability, getting top performance from his incredible talent. If he had been a national hero in the early twenties, now he was even more so—the most photographed, the most written about, the most talked about, and the most popular person in the nation.

He didn't become a plaster saint, by any means. He still spent plenty of time at various pleasure domes—like the House of the Good Shepherd—in the various American League cities he visited in the course of his labors. And he didn't become a teetotaler either, despite the Eighteenth Amendment.

But he never forgot his origins and he spent lots of time visiting children in hospitals and orphanages.

"To really know what sort of man Ruth was," sportswriter Tom Meany once said, "you have to understand that his affection for children was sincere. The Babe, for all of his lusty living, for all of his bluff and often crude ways, had ever a soft spot in his heart for kids. Every public appearance Ruth made, in his playing days or thereafter, was an inconvenience and an annoyance, but Babe never once turned down a request to go somewhere and visit kids unless it was because he had a previous obligation to visit kids somewhere else."

Author Paul Gallico always did tend toward hyperbole, but there is still a grain of truth in his description of Ruth's visit to the hospital room of a sick boy—his name was Johnny Sylvester—who had just had a serious operation and had apparently lost the will to live. As might be expected, Babe Ruth was Johnny's idol. A reporter mentioned to Ruth that a visit from him might help, and the next morning there he was. It wasn't unique; it was a scene repeated countless times.

In Paul Gallico's words: "The door opened and it was God Himself who walked into the room, straight from His glittering throne, God dressed in a camel's hair polo coat and a flat, camel's hair cap, God with a flat nose and little piggy eyes, a big grin, and a fat black cigar sticking out of the side of it."

The Babe sat down next to the boy whose life was in danger and talked with him, answered questions, gave him a baseball bat—saying he expected the boy would soon be well enough to use it—and an autographed baseball. He also promised young Johnny Sylvester that he would hit a home run for him that afternoon at Yankee Stadium (which indeed he did!).

The sequel to this story is that Johnny Sylvester began to improve after Ruth's visit. Twenty years later, when Ruth himself was gravely ill, thirty-year-old Johnny Sylvester returned the visit, bringing with him his most cherished possession: the autographed baseball Ruth had given him two decades earlier.

It is also characteristic of Ruth that throughout his life he identified publicly with St. Mary's Industrial School for Boys, in part an orphanage but even more a reformatory. Many people with similar backgrounds who subsequently became well known have hastily invented a more respectable upbringing. If he was anything at all, though, Ruth was genuine and unpretentious; it is doubtful if the thought ever entered his mind.

In 1919 much of St. Mary's was destroyed by fire. That summer, on an off-day, Ruth pitched an exhibition game in Baltimore to help raise funds to rebuild the school. In 1920, in a continued effort to raise money, Ruth escorted the school's fifty-piece band around the American League as the boys went on tour with the Yankees; they performed before Yankee games and then passed the hat to collect money for the school. They also gave evening concerts at which the Babe would appear and make the principal appeal for money. They always displayed a large banner which read:

BABE RUTH'S BOYS BAND

DO YOUR BIT TO HELP REBUILD THE SCHOOL
THAT MADE BABE RUTH FAMOUS

He frequently donated automobiles to St. Mary's, for the use of the Brothers. Once, when Brother Matthias was in New York, Ruth pointed to an expensive car in an automobile showroom and asked, "Do you think I should buy that car, Brother?"

"If you think you can afford it, George."

The next day the car was delivered to the hotel where Brother Matthias was staying, with a brief note: "With thanks for everything that you and St. Mary's have done for me."

A few months later, Brother Matthias had an accident in which he was not hurt but the car was destroyed. Upon hearing about it, Ruth promptly had another one delivered to St. Mary's.

Harry Hooper, Ruth's teammate in Boston in 1914 and the man who convinced Ed Barrow that Ruth should be changed from a pitcher to an outfielder, was still playing in the American League in the mid-twenties. Later, he coached baseball at Princeton University. He was an intelligent observer of the world around him.

"I saw it all happen, from beginning to end," Hooper recalled a number of years later. "But sometimes I still can't believe what I saw: this nineteen-year-old kid, poorly educated, only lightly brushed by the social veneer we call civilization, gradually transformed into the idol of American youth and the symbol of baseball the world over—a man loved by more people and with an intensity of feeling that perhaps has never been equaled before or since. I saw a man transformed from a human being into something pretty close to a god. If somebody had predicted that on the Boston Red Sox back in 1914, he would have been thrown into a lunatic asylum."

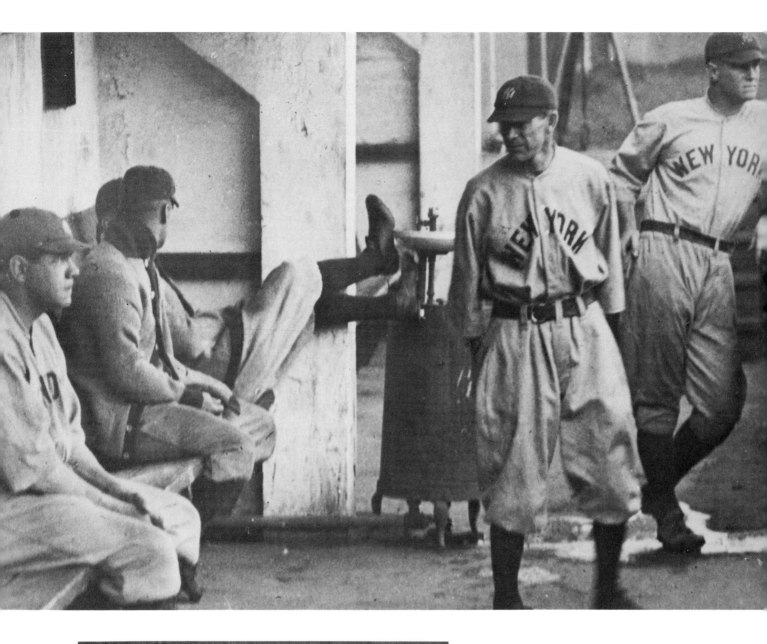

Ruth and Yankee Manager Miller Huggins (facing Ruth) never did think much of each other. It is the summer of 1925 and they are nearing a showdown. All the others in the dugout (including first baseman Wally Pipp, standing) are obviously trying to put some kind of distance between themselves and the two adversaries.

On August 29, in St. Louis, Huggins finally suspended his star slugger without pay and fined him $5,000 for good measure.

A distraught Ruth arrives in New York. He has been sent home from St. Louis by Manager Huggins.

Ruth was reinstated on September 7, after apologizing to the manager and promising to mend his ways. Huggins and Ruth shake hands and try to smile for the photographer.

The winter of 1925–26 was devoted to getting back into condition once again. This time, however, working out at Artie McGovern's gym takes precedence over cutting timber in the country. Above, Artie himself is on the left.

Below, two other regulars at McGovern's gym: band leader Paul Whiteman (left), and composer John Philip Sousa (right).

Prior workouts at McGovern's didn't make spring training any less of an ordeal for the Babe.

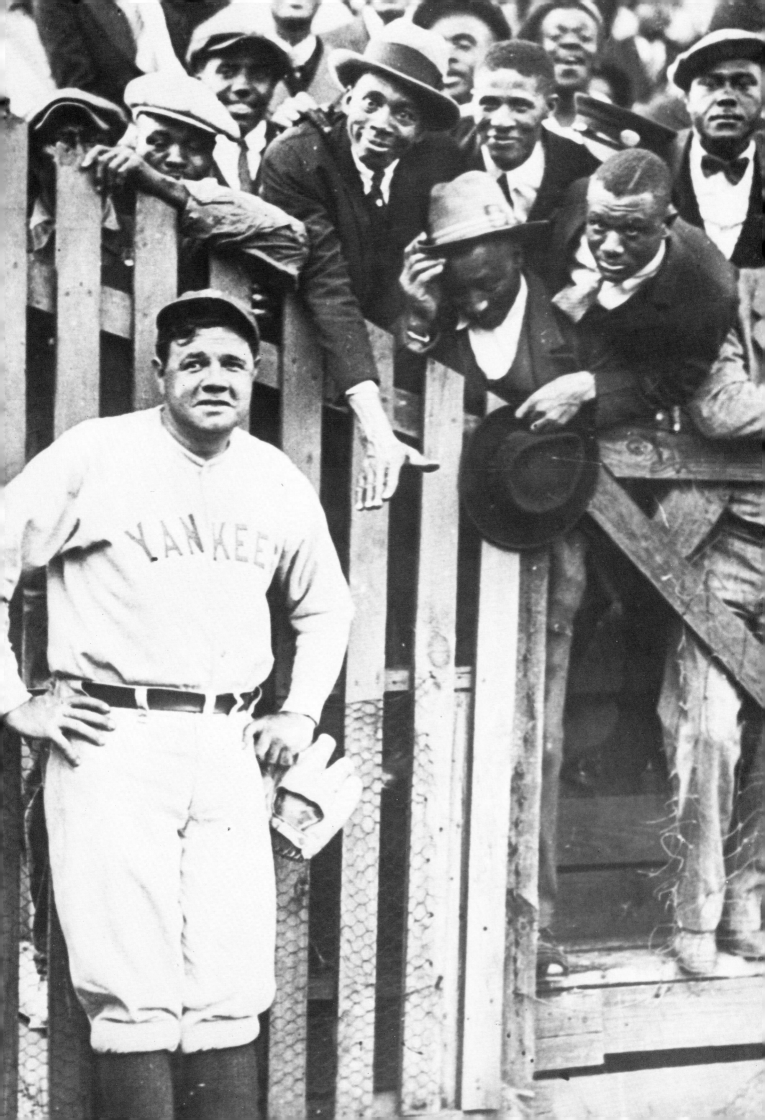

LEFT: In Ruth's day, after spring training in Florida the Yankees made their way north to New York by train, stopping frequently en route for exhibition games. All Southern towns had segregated seating at the ballparks, usually confining blacks to a partitioned section of the bleachers.

Ruth and Rogers Hornsby of the St. Louis Cardinals compare bats. Hornsby, generally considered the greatest right-handed hitter of all time, batted over .400 in 1922, 1924, and 1925. In his off-year, 1923, he slipped all the way to .384.

Ruth and Hornsby before the 1926 World Series. The baby is Christy Walsh, Jr., age five months, and his proud mother isn't letting him out of her sight.

Also at the '26 World Series (left to right) sportswriter Fred Lieb, Ruth, John McGraw, Miller Huggins, ex-pitcher Nick Altrock, Rogers Hornsby, and Christy Walsh. Fred Lieb is the man who first called Yankee Stadium "the House That Ruth Built."

Ruth hit three home runs in the fourth game of the '26 Series. This is his third, off Cardinal pitcher Hi Bell. The catcher is Bob O'Farrell.

The next day, the Chevrolet agency across the street from the ballpark took note of the accomplishment: the cracked glass below the Babe's image indicates where one of his drives landed.

147

After the 1926 World Series, Babe went on tour as a single in vaudeville, starting in Minneapolis and ending in California three months later.

Lefty Hub Pruett of the St. Louis Browns. He lost more games than he won, but if he could have fooled everyone in the batter's box the way he fooled Ruth he would rank with Walter Johnson and Christy Mathewson. Ruth struck out 13 times in his first 17 official times at bat against Pruett.

After his baseball career ended, Pruett became a doctor. On meeting the Babe a number of years later, Pruett thanked Ruth for indirectly helping pay his way through medical school.

Not used to pitchers thanking him for anything, much less for boosting their standard of living, Ruth could only mumble a few words like "It was my pleasure" or something to that effect.

The Ruthian batting swing, photographed in 1927, a sequence that was closely analyzed and debated by fans and players alike. Ruth's swing clearly has an upward arc, in contrast to the level parallel-to-the-ground swing that was favored by most batting authorities at the time.

Behind the batting cage, Ruth and Gehrig watch a teammate take batting practice. In 1927 Ruth hit 60 home runs, Gehrig 47. They remained the top one-two for homers on one team in a single season until Maris walloped 61 and Mantle 54 for the Yankees in 1961.

The argument over whether a batter should swing at the ball slightly upward, level, or even slightly downward continues to this day.

Lou, Babe, and Lady Amco (a chicken).

Whatever Mr. Ruth is saying into that radio microphone has everyone amused except, apparently, Mr. Gehrig.

The launching of home run number 60 on September 30, 1927, off Tom Zachary of the Washington Senators. The catcher is Muddy Ruel and the umpire is Bill Dinneen.

Crossing home plate makes number 60 official for a new home run record. Lou Gehrig is the first to congratulate Ruth, with Yankee batboy Eddie Bennett close behind. The catcher is still Muddy Ruel and the umpire Bill Dinneen.

This is perhaps the most widely reproduced of all team pictures, simply because the 1927 Yankees are often called the greatest team of all time. Nevertheless, as a team photo it has its peculiarities. For instance, Don Miller, in the back row between Ruth and Meusel, never played a game as a Yankee and wasn't even on the roster. He just happened to be at the Stadium that day for a tryout. And why there should be an "unknown" (back row, one in from the right end) on such a well-known team remains a mystery to this day! One authority, Gordon Fleming, claims that "unknown" is really a batting-practice pitcher named Joe Styborski, but others are dubious.

1927 NEW YORK YANKEES   WORLD CHAMPIONS

FRONT ROW: Julie Wera, Mike Gazella, Pat Collins, Eddie Bennett (Mascot), Benny Bengough, Ray Morehart, Myles Thomas, Cedric Durst. MIDDLE ROW: Urban Shocker, Joe Dugan, Earle Combs, Charlie O'Leary (Coach), Miller Huggins (Manager), Art Fletcher (Coach), Mark Koenig, Dutch Ruether, Johnny Grabowski, George Pipgras. BACK ROW: Lou Gehrig, Herb Pennock, Tony Lazzeri, Wiley Moore, Babe Ruth, Don Miller, Bob Meusel, Bob Shawkey, Waite Hoyt, Joe Giard, Ben Paschal, (Unknown), Doc Wood (Trainer).

LEFT: Ruth's periodic salary battles with Colonel Ruppert were invariably given extensive press coverage. Eventually, though, the two always sat down and signed on the dotted line — this time with Ed Barrow looking over their shoulders.

BELOW: Ruth's biweekly paycheck in 1927, when his annual salary was $70,000. (By coincidence, the check is dated September 30, the day he hit number 60.)

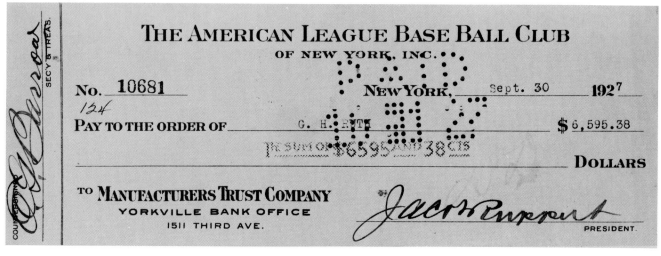

Christy Walsh and Babe Ruth. After the 1927 season ended, Ruth and Gehrig embarked on a lengthy barnstorming tour—the Bustin' Babes vs. the Larrupin' Lous.

BELOW: Gehrig, Walsh, and Ruth, top row center. The tour covered twenty-one cities in nine states and drew a quarter of a million paying customers.

Stars available for
Personal Appearance, Merchandise Endorsements,
Exhibition Baseball Games, Vaudeville, Moving Pictures,
Talking Pictures, Radio and all forms of Commercial contracts

Under

CHRISTY WALSH MANAGEMENT

570 SEVENTH AVENUE, NEW YORK CITY

Eventually Christy Walsh built up quite a business.

Some lucky youngsters were able to get their pictures taken with the Babe.

Cities often made Ruth their acting superintendent of police as he passed through. He always put on the uniform and played the role to the hilt.

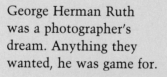

George Herman Ruth was a photographer's dream. Anything they wanted, he was game for.

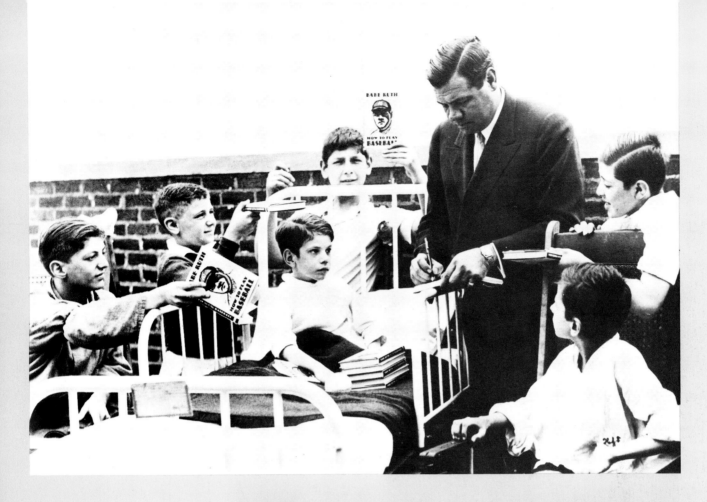

As usual, stops at hospitals punctuated his travels.

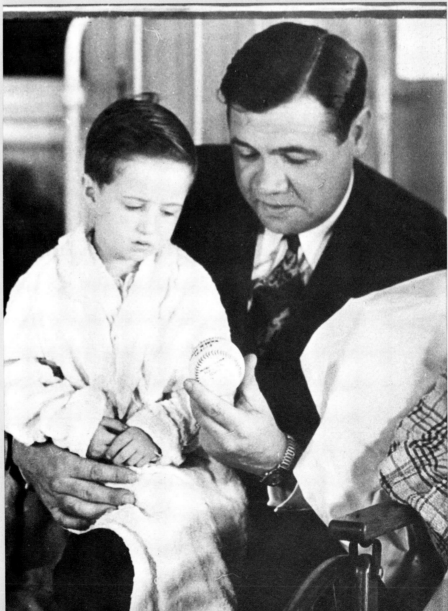

161

Wherever he went and whatever he did, the man was always surrounded by children.

162

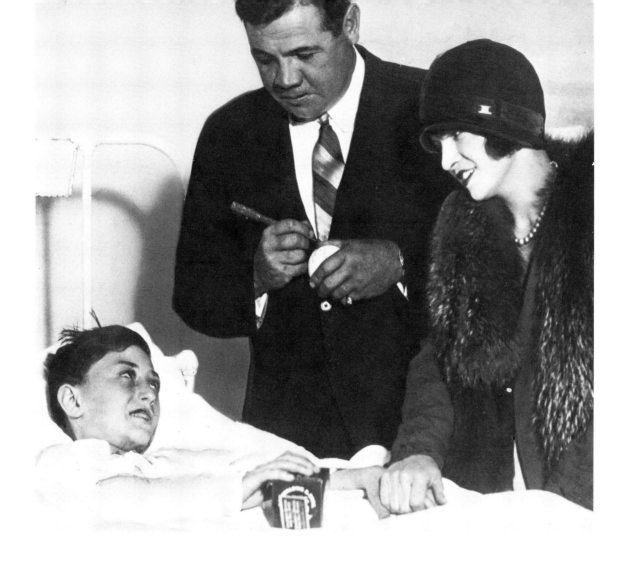

The story of Johnny Sylvester is the most often told of Ruth's hospital visits. Views differ on whether its commercialization was (a) vulgar, (b) gross, (c) in bad taste, or (d) all of the above.

"This one's for you, Johnny"

The specter of death had been in 11-year-old Johnny Sylvester's eyes that morning when, in answer to an urgent message, "The Babe" visited him in the hospital. Ruth had given Johnny an autographed baseball, and asked, "Will you get well if I hit a homer, just for you, in the World Series?" The stricken boy nodded a hopeful promise.

This is the dramatic background for that now famous episode—Babe Ruth confidently standing at the plate, and smashing a home run—just for young Johnny Sylvester.

Johnny had his ball, autographed by "The Babe" personally, and lived, never to forget that the mighty Yankee had hit a home run, just for him.

Your business correspondence may never save a life, but your letters are sure to make a favorable impression if they're typed on Gilbert Bond—the quality standard of the entire industry. Unrivalled for that crisp "banknote" feel, Gilbert New Cotton Fibre Content Bond announces to everyone that your company is "quality."

Your local printer or Gilbert paper merchant will be happy to give you samples of Gilbert writing papers.

GILBERT
PAPER COMPANY

MENASHA, WISCONSIN

With Notre Dame football coach Knute Rockne. The Babe — dressed for the occasion, as always — gets some instruction on the finer points of the sport.

A football dinner. (Left to right) Stanford coach Pop Warner, Babe Ruth, Knute Rockne, Christy Walsh, Lou Gehrig, and USC coach Howard Jones.

Sartorial elegance.

LEFT: The famous photograph of Ruth by Nickolas Muray, taken around 1927.

Four other poses snapped by the photographer at the same time.

RIGHT: The year 1928 was a presidential election year—Republican Herbert Hoover vs. Democratic candidate Al Smith—and Ruth made no secret of his sympathies.

BELOW: Nor did a number of other sports personalities, from Yankee batboy and mascot Eddie Bennett to heavyweight boxing champion Gene Tunney.

BABE RUTH WEARS THE BROWN DERBY

Babe Ruth, home run king of baseball fame, true to his Roman Catholic teachings and his education in a papal parochial school, is campaigning for his co-religionist, Al Smith, for President.

Incidentally, Ruth is a Knight of Columbus—"brother" of Al's. At the opening of the campaign some photographer at the ball park in Washington, D. C., tried to get Ruth to pose for a picture with Herbert Hoover, but Ruth refused, saying it was "politics." Of course, its not politics for him to campaign for Al Smith—that's religion.

ABOVE: As Election Day approached, the infighting became vicious. This circular accuses Ruth of supporting Al Smith because they are both Catholics.

RIGHT: Despite Ruth's efforts, Herbert Hoover won the election. Thus Al Smith could subsequently enjoy a carefree game of golf with the Babe—instead of worrying about how to stop the Depression that began shortly after Hoover entered the White House.

A typical Ruthian offense.

There are literally hundreds of photographs of Ruth similar to this one — the classic climax at the end of his typical home run swing. It probably represents the most common image of Ruth in the public mind. This particular photograph is unique, however, in that it served as

the model for the Babe Ruth commemorative postage stamp issued by the United States Government on July 6, 1983.

Did He Really Call His Shot?

1928-1932

In the early months of 1929, far-reaching changes took place in Babe Ruth's private life, assuming, of course, that any part of his fishbowl existence could be considered private.

On the night of January 11, 1929, at the age of thirty-one, Helen Woodford Ruth—Mrs. Babe Ruth—died of burns and suffocation from a fire that started accidentally while she was asleep in her home in Watertown, Massachusetts. The fire was caused by defective electrical wiring recently installed when the house was remodeled. Eight-year-old Dorothy was away at boarding school in Wellesley at the time. The Ruths had been separated since 1925.

Actually, it took a while before the police realized that the deceased was Mrs. Babe Ruth. Neighbors had known her as Mrs. Edward H. Kinder, the wife of a dentist. Helen and Dr. Kinder had been living together as husband and wife in the Watertown house since 1927. It was a full day before her true identity became known.

Although they had not lived together for more than three years, both Babe and Helen had religious objections to terminating their marriage by divorce. This was despite the facts that Helen was living with Dr. Kinder and that as far back as 1923 Babe had met someone in whom he was seriously interested. Her name was Claire Hodgson (née Merritt), a pretty and brainy young widow from Georgia who had come to New York in 1920 with her three-year-old daughter, Julia.

Claire made her living as an illustrators' model with occasional small parts on the stage and in the movies. She was introduced to the Babe in 1923 and they soon fell in love. With Helen and the Babe, it had been all of three months between meeting and marrying; with Claire, it took six years.

Helen's tragic death allowed Claire and Babe finally to marry. They did so on April 17, 1929, at the Roman Catholic Church of St. Gregory the Great at 140 West Ninetieth Street. Babe was thirty-four years of age; Claire, twenty-eight (she was born on September 11, 1900). Although they had arranged for the ceremony to be performed before 6 A.M. in order to have some privacy, the news got around. By the time they left the church, thousands of people had gathered in the street outside and a small army of photographers and reporters was pleased to join them for breakfast in their new eleven-room apartment, which occupied the entire seventh floor at 345 West Eighty-eighth Street, between West End Avenue and Riverside Drive. Claire's mother lived in the same building.

(Babe and Claire lived there for several years and then moved a block away to 173 Riverside Drive, at the corner of Eighty-ninth Street. In 1942 they moved, for the last time, to an eleven-room apartment overlooking the Hudson River at 110 Riverside Drive, at the corner of Eighty-third Street. The Babe stayed at half a dozen places during the three decades he was in New York City—from the Ansonia in the early twenties to 110 Riverside Drive in the forties—most of which were within a few blocks of one another on Manhattan's polyglot Upper West Side. He almost always lived somewhere between Seventieth and Ninetieth streets, bounded by Broadway on the east and Riverside Drive on the west.)

Marriage meant instant family, for suddenly the Babe had got himself not only a wife, but two young daughters as well. In 1930 he and Claire formally adopted both Dorothy (nine) and Julia (thirteen)—that is, Claire adopted Dorothy and Babe simultaneously adopted Julia. With two daughters, he began calling Claire "Mom" in their presence, and as time passed, that increasingly became his name for her. Perhaps it was because she mothered him as much as she mothered Dorothy and Julia. Not that it was so surprising—after all, he'd never really had a "Mom" before.

Soon after the wedding, Claire started accompanying Babe on his road trips with the Yankees. It isn't clear who first suggested this arrangement—Colonel Ruppert, the Babe, or Claire—but apparently it made everyone happy (except the other Yankee wives). Although wives were not allowed on the road as a matter of club policy, in this particular instance (and this instance only) Colonel Ruppert was delighted to make an exception. Ruth was a world-class hell-raiser away from home; if having Claire along helped cut down on his extracurricular activities, so much the better.

The two of them had a private compartment on the Yankees' train (baseball teams didn't travel by air until the late forties) and always had their own hotel suite, where they took all their meals by room service. This was a necessity, not an indulgence: the Babe's presence in any restaurant or hotel dining room was guaranteed to completely disrupt service. Claire, who was well aware of the value of a dollar, always thought it pretty cheap of the Yankees to deduct her travel and hotel expenses from her husband's biweekly paycheck.

That paycheck had grown considerably over the years. When the Babe's five-year, $52,000-a-year contract ran out, it was replaced in early 1927 by a three-year agreement for $70,000 a year. (The average salary of a major league ballplayer in those days was about $7,000.) In March of 1930 he hit his all-time high, a two-year contract calling for an astronomical (for that era) salary of $80,000 a year.

March of 1930 was barely five months after the infamous stock market crash of October 1929. The Great Depression was just around the corner. It may be true or it may be apocryphal, but someone reportedly asked Ruth whether he thought it was right that he should make $80,000 a year, more money than Herbert Hoover, the President of the United States. President Hoover's salary was $75,000.

"Why not?" Ruth is said to have answered. "I had a better year than he did."

In addition, the Babe typically made double his Yankee salary annually from endorsements, postseason barnstorming tours, and a variety of other activities arranged for him by Christy Walsh. His Yankee salary plus his outside gross must have added up to $240,000 a year in 1930 and 1931. After Walsh's cut and income taxes, which were minimal in those days, the Babe probably took home about 75 percent of it: $180,000 per annum, not bad for the thirties, when "Brother, Can You Spare a Dime?" was the theme song of the times.

Claire didn't try to remake the Babe into someone he wasn't, but neither did she hesitate to bring her influence to bear where she thought necessary: "Now that I was Mrs. Ruth, I felt Mrs. Ruth had a job to do. I had a few reforms to institute."

One of her first "reforms" had to do with Babe's eating habits—with those prodigious pig-outs that were as much a part of the legend as his skyscraper pop-ups, his whirling-dervish strikeouts, and his booming over-the-stadium-roof homers. Sometimes it seemed as though the Babe overindulged more to make an impression than to satisfy his appetite.

Pitcher Paul Derringer, for example, claimed he once had breakfast with Ruth, and he still appeared shaken when he recalled the incident thirty years later: "I was in the dining car, and the seat opposite me was the only one empty. In came Ruth, alone, and seeing the empty chair he sat down at my table. The Babe called over the waiter and ordered a pitcher of ice, a pint of ginger ale, a porterhouse steak, garnished with four fried eggs, fried potatoes, and a pot of coffee. A few minutes later the waiter set the pitcher of ice and pint of ginger ale in front of Ruth. The Babe pulled a pint of bourbon out of his hip pocket, poured it over the ice, poured the ginger ale, shook up the mixture, and that was his breakfast juice. After that, he attacked the steak, the eggs, and the potatoes."

One cannot help thinking that Ruth was showing off for Derringer. But whether he was or not, Claire successfully redirected his eating habits along more approved dietary lines. She reduced his intake of junk food, desserts, and soda pop in favor of meat, vegetables, and milk. He continued to eat a steak for breakfast, but lunch became a light sandwich and milk. And instead of another steak and a few beers before bedtime, she persuaded him to substitute a club sandwich and another glass or two of milk.

The new Mrs. Ruth also outlawed scotch, bourbon, and other hard liquor during the baseball season. From April through September, the Babe drank nothing stronger than beer. And all social events, without exception, were subject to a strict ten o'clock curfew.

To the surprise of many of his old nocturnal drinking buddies, no one ever heard the Babe complain about his conservative new life-style. Instead, he seemed happier than ever, no doubt partly because he was no longer a frolicsome youngster—he was, after all, in his mid-thirties and many wild oats had already been sown—and partly because he and Claire and the children were truly devoted to one another and enjoyed one another's company.

In 1929, '30, and '31, the Bambino continued his torrid hitting, leading the league in home runs each season. But New York finished behind the pennant-winning Philadelphia Athletics all three years. To some extent, it was because their diminutive manager, Miller Huggins, died during the 1929 season. Only fifty years old, Huggins went into the hospital on September 20 and died of erysipelas, a rare skin disease, less than a week later.

In 1931, at the age of thirty-six, the Babe either led the league or was runner-up in home runs, runs batted in, batting average, slugging average, total bases, and bases on balls. It was his last great year. But it was not his last great scene.

As he had ever since 1926, Ruth spent considerable time in late 1931 and early 1932 working with Artie McGovern at his gymnasium. By February of 1932, when he left for spring training, he was down to a respectable 225 pounds, not bad for a thirty-seven-year-old who could put on 5 pounds just by walking past a chocolate layer cake. In the early thirties, his weight tended to fluctuate between 225 and 245 pounds over the course of a season.

The 1932 season would be his eighteenth full year in the big leagues. Subsequently he would play two more full seasons in the majors, making twenty in all, a truly remarkable achievement for someone who in the first eleven of those years had gone to astonishing lengths to break every training and conditioning rule ever promulgated.

At the start of the 1932 season, Ruth took the first pay cut of his life. Despite the fact that he had batted .373 in 1931, Ruppert insisted that he take a $10,000 reduction in salary. They finally compromised on a $5,000 cut—a one-year contract for $75,000 plus 25 percent of the net receipts from Yankee exhibition games.

Under the leadership of Joe McCarthy—in his sophomore year as manager—the Yankees won their first pennant since 1928. Their World Series opponents were the Chicago Cubs, first-place finishers by a narrow margin in the National League. The 1928 Series had been Ruth's crowning glory: he had blasted three home runs in the fourth and final game and batted .625 for the Series as a whole. It hardly seemed possible that he could surpass that in 1932.

But surpass it he did.

What he did, in the fifth inning of the third game, with the count two balls and two strikes, is probably the single best-remembered, most glorified feat in all of World Series history—indeed, in all of baseball history. Under the most dramatic of circumstances, with a hostile crowd screaming epithets at him and the Chicago Cubs taunting him as a fat over-the-hill has-been, Ruth pointed to the center field bleachers and, on the next pitch, walloped a tremendous home run with the ball soaring high above the very spot to which he had just pointed. It was the longest home run that had ever been hit in Chicago's Wrigley Field.

It was Ruth's second home run of the game and it effectively squashed any remaining Chicago hopes. The Yankees went on to sweep the Series with four straight victories, their third World Series sweep in a row (1927, '28, and '32).

But the nagging question has dragged on for more than half a century: Did he *really* call his shot? Did the man actually have the audacity to point to the center field bleachers and leave himself open to the ridicule he would have received had he struck out or popped up? What a laughingstock he would have been!

The reason the question refuses to go away is because eyewitnesses themselves cannot agree on what happened. Did he call his shot or didn't he? The answer depends on whom you ask.

Even newspaper accounts of the game are inconclusive. Most papers didn't say anything at all about his pointing to center field. But Joe Williams in the *New York World-Telegram* wrote that "with the Cubs riding him unmercifully from the bench, Ruth pointed to center and punched a screaming liner to a spot where no ball had ever been hit before." And John Drebinger's story in *The New York Times* mentioned that "in no mistaken motions, the Babe notified the crowd that the nature of his retaliation would be a wallop right out of the confines of the park."

Sportswriter Tom Meany, who was in the press box at the time, went into the incident in some detail in his biography of Ruth: "It was the most defiant, and the most debated, gesture in World Series history. Chicago pitcher Charlie Root threw a called strike past the Babe and the Cub bench let the big fellow have it. Babe, holding the bat in one hand, held up the index finger of the other to signify that it was indeed a strike. Root threw another called strike. Ruth held up two fingers and the Cub bench howled in derision.

"It was then that the big fellow made what many believe to be the *beau geste* of his entire career. He pointed in the direction of dead center field. Some say it was merely a gesture toward Root, others say he was just letting the Cub bench know that he still had the big one left. Ruth himself has changed his version a couple of times but the reaction of most of those who saw him point his finger toward center field is that he was calling his shot. Everybody agrees that Babe did point in the direction of center field and that he did hit a home run there and that's good enough for me."

Ruth himself, of course, agreed that he did indeed call his shot: "I swung from the ground with everything I had . . . and that ball just went on and on and on and hit far up in the center field bleachers in exactly the spot I had pointed to."

Other true believers:

George Pipgras, Yankee pitcher: "Yes, sir, he called it. He pointed toward the bleachers and then he hit it right there. I saw him do it."

Joe Sewell, Yankee third baseman: "I was there. I saw it. I don't care what anybody says. He called it."

Lefty Gomez, Yankee pitcher: "Ruth pointed with his bat in his right hand, to right field, not center field. But he definitely called his shot."

Lou Gehrig, Yankee first baseman: "What do you think of the nerve of that big monkey? Calling his shot and getting away with it."

Pat Pieper, Wrigley Field public address announcer, who was seated a short distance from Ruth: "Don't let anybody tell you differently. Babe definitely pointed to center field."

But the skeptics:

Charlie Root, Cub pitcher: "Ruth did *not* point at the fence before he swung. If he'd made a gesture like that, I'd have put one in his ear and knocked him on his ass."

Billy Herman, Cub second baseman: "What Ruth did was hold up his hand to say that he only had two strikes on him, that he had another one coming. But he was pointing out toward Charlie Root, not toward the center field bleachers."

Burleigh Grimes, Cub pitcher: "He never called it. Forget it."

Charlie Grimm, Cub manager and first baseman: "He didn't call his shot. He was shouting to pitcher Guy Bush, who was in our dugout. Bush was his chief heckler and he was yelling to Bush that he'd like to see him out there pitching. As he yelled that to Bush, he pointed toward the pitcher's mound."

Gabby Hartnett, Cub catcher: "Babe waved his hand across the plate toward our bench, which was on the third base side. One finger was up. I think only the umpire and I heard him say, 'It only takes one to hit it.' He didn't point out at the bleachers. If he had, I'd be the first to say so."

So after all is said and done, we are no nearer the answer than we were before. Eyewitness testimony is of no help because it cancels itself out. Did George Washington ever tell a lie? Did he really throw a silver dollar across the Rappahannock River? Was Sherlock Holmes a figment of Sir Arthur Conan Doyle's imagination or did he actually live in London at 221B Baker Street? Was Johnny Appleseed real or mythical? What about John Henry? Like it or not, whether the Babe did or didn't call his shot has moved beyond the domain of fact and evidence into the realm of myth and legend.

The year 1928 is no different from any other year
so far as Babe Ruth is concerned: his time is
consumed by autographing baseballs, by
youngsters, or by both at once.

Ruth was a heavy smoker, a habit he could never break. He smoked cigarettes (occasionally), a pipe (frequently), and cigars (always), including while playing pool . . .

. . . as well as when hitting fungoes (no mean trick) . . .

. . . but not while playing the saxophone for an unappreciative Lou Gehrig.

In 1928 Ruth and Gehrig tied for the runs-batted-in leadership of the American League, with 142 RBIs apiece. No one else was even close.

Four of the greatest on the 1926, '27, and '28 pennant-winning Yankees. Left to right: Lou Gehrig, center fielder Earle Combs, second baseman Tony Lazzeri, and the Bambino.

Ruth and Gehrig at Dexter Park in Brooklyn for an exhibition game in October 1928. They are also advertising a rodeo that will soon appear in Madison Square Garden.

The Sultan of Swat is awarded an M.S. degree in hitting (Master of Swat). In the front row, left to right: Miller Huggins, St. Louis Browns batting star George Sisler, Commissioner Landis, Ruth, sportswriter Cy Sanborn, and Colonel Ruppert.

The coffin of Helen Ruth is being carried into a Boston funeral parlor. Separated from the Babe since about 1925, Helen had been living in Watertown, Massachusetts, as the wife of a dentist, Edward H. Kinder. She died of suffocation due to a fire in her Watertown home on January 11, 1929. She was only thirty-one. At Helen's burial, the Babe stands between Helen's sister, Josephine, and her mother, Mrs. Joanna Woodford.

Ruth and Manager Miller Huggins at spring training in 1929. The year 1929 was laced with tragedy. Helen's death in January was followed by the equally unexpected death of Huggins in September, at the age of fifty.

ABOVE LEFT: Claire Hodgson in 1923, at about the time she first met Mr. Ruth. ABOVE: Claire in 1912 in Athens, Georgia, at the age of twelve.

LEFT: Actor James Barton, the man who introduced Babe to Claire. Jimmy Barton became famous when he starred in *Tobacco Road*, one of the longest-running plays in the history of the Broadway theater. (It ran 3,182 performances, from its opening in 1933 until it finally closed in 1941.)

Babe and Claire in April 1929, shortly before their marriage.

The wedding ceremony took place on April 17, 1929, shortly before six o'clock in the morning. Now it is later that same day.

The newlyweds at Yankee
Stadium on the following day,
April 18, Opening Day of the
1929 season.

BELOW: It is the 1929 Opening
Day game at Yankee Stadium
on April 18, Yankees vs. Red
Sox, and the Bambino is
presenting a wedding present to
his bride — a home run into the
left field seats in his first time
at bat. As he rounded second
base in his home run trot, Babe
doffed his cap to Claire with an
exaggerated flourish. (The
pitcher was Red Ruffing, the
catcher was Charlie Berry, and
the umpire was Bill McGowan.)

LEFT: With daughter
Dorothy (on his knee)
and Julia (Claire's
daughter by a previous
marriage) in 1930.
Dorothy is nine years old
and Julia is thirteen.

BELOW: (Left to right:)
Claire, Dorothy, Julia,
and the Babe. Babe and
Claire are signing papers
in October of 1930,
officially making
Dorothy and Julia their
legally adopted
daughters.

Yankee third baseman Red Rolfe (on the left), the Babe, and reserve infielder Don Heffner.

Somebody must have liked Babe Ruth movies, because he was always being asked to make more of them. P.S. It wasn't the critics.

The Ruth family in January of 1931 — left to right, Dorothy, Claire, Babe, and Julia — with a special kiss for Dorothy.

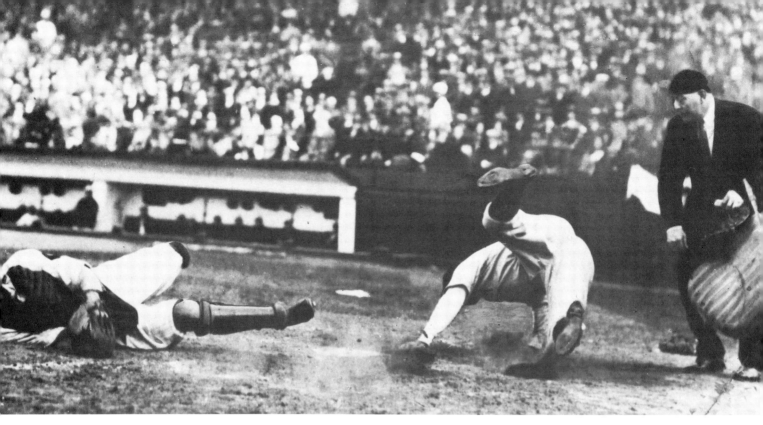

The Babe was an aggressive base runner throughout his career and he didn't let up as he grew older. Here on April 22, 1931 – Opening Day in Fenway Park – at the age of thirty-six, Ruth barrels into Boston catcher Charlie Berry, an ex–All-American football player, as Babe scores from third on a sacrifice fly to short right field. The umpire is Bill Guthrie.

BELOW: It is still April 22, the bottom half of the same inning, and the collision finally takes its toll. Babe has collapsed in the outfield while running after a fly ball. He is being carried off the field. His ailment was diagnosed as a strained ligament in his left thigh.

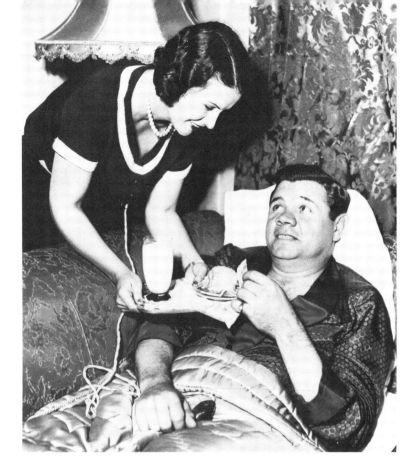

April 29, a week later, and Claire is babying her husband as he recuperates at home.

On the rubbing table in the trainer's room, while Lou Gehrig sympathizes.

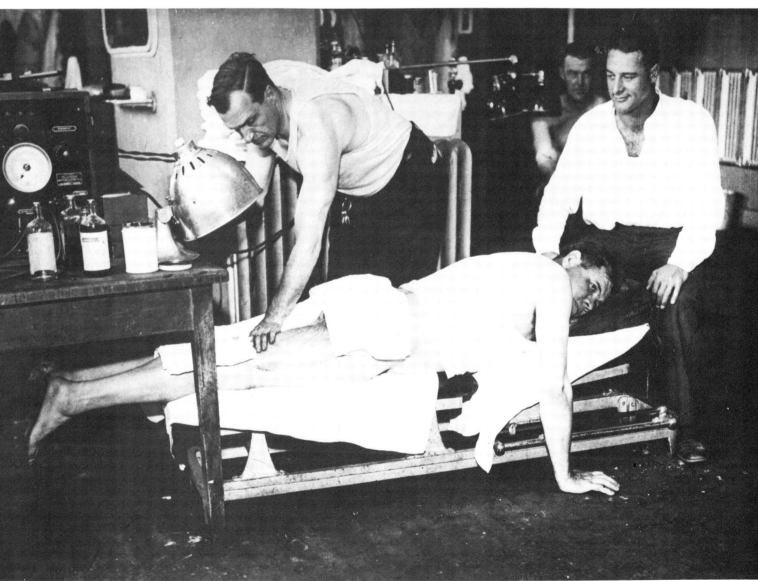

Being carried off the field was old hat to the Babe. Here he's knocked himself cold running into the outfield wall while chasing a fly ball in Washington's Griffith Stadium.

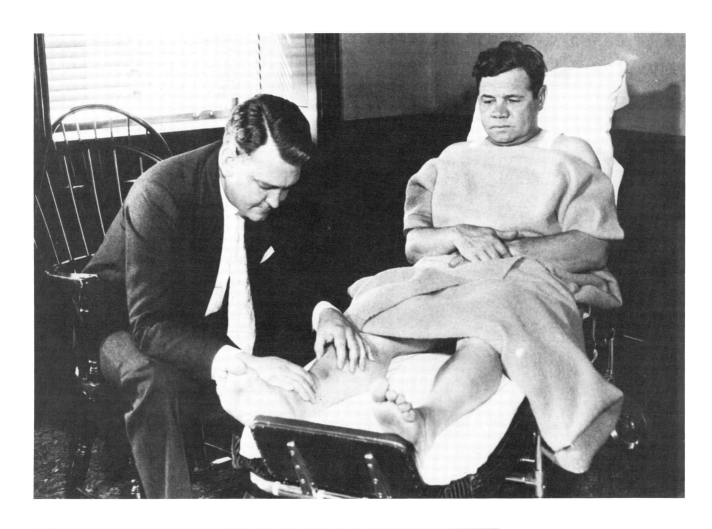

ABOVE: This time it's a badly bruised right leg. While running from first base to second he was struck by a batted ball hit by Lou Gehrig.

LEFT: Babe and Claire arriving early for the Army–Notre Dame football game in November of 1931.

RIGHT: Cincinnati pitcher Paul Derringer. The Babe's gastronomical proclivities left him flabbergasted.

BELOW: Yankee Manager Joe McCarthy and the Babe. In 1931, two years after the death of Miller Huggins, Joe McCarthy took over the managerial reins of the Yankees. But Ruth didn't like McCarthy any more than he'd liked Huggins — especially since the Babe now wanted the job for himself. Ruth and McCarthy never spoke off the field and said as little as possible to each other on it.

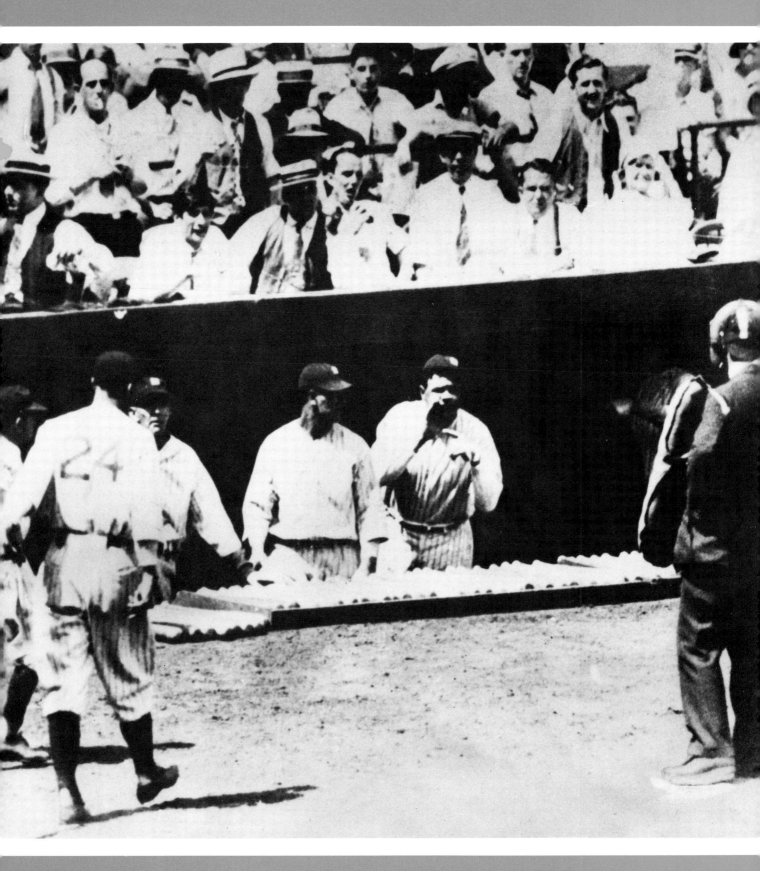

Speaking of dislikes, the Babe was never overly fond of umpires either. Here he is in a typical lifetime stance vis-à-vis all authority figures, except for Brother Matthias. (Number 24 is Sammy Bryd — "Babe Ruth's legs" — returning to the dugout after apparently taking a called third strike.)

ABOVE: With Hack
Wilson, who hit 56 home
runs in 1930. Five feet
six inches tall and 195
pounds, Hack also had
the astonishing total of
190 runs batted in that
year.

LEFT: Pitcher Charlie
Root of the Cubs. Did
Ruth call his shot against
Root in the third game of
the 1932 World Series or
didn't he? According to
Root, who was a tough
cookie, "Ruth did *not*
point at the fence before
he swung. If he'd made a
gesture like that, I'd have
put one in his ear and
knocked him on his ass."

These remarkable pictures – reproduced from 16 mm home movie film – were taken by a spectator (Matt Kandle, Sr.) at the very moment of Ruth's "called shot." The first frame shows Ruth definitely pointing. But at what? At pitcher Charlie Root? At someone on the Cubs' bench (which was on the third base side of the infield)? Or was it at the center field fence? The second frame, taken a couple of minutes later, shows Ruth connecting with the next pitch. The ball is already on its way toward the center field bleachers.

An elated Babe Ruth has just crossed home plate after hitting the most celebrated home run of his life. He is being congratulated by an admiring Lou Gehrig (who, even though no one remembers, followed with a home run of his own). Everyone reacted in their own fashion. Catcher Gabby Hartnett seems stunned while umpire Roy Van Graflan appears somewhat amused.

"How Can You Manage the Yankees When You Can't Even Manage Yourself?"

1933-1935

Babe Ruth got the managerial bug after the death of Miller Huggins in 1929. That fall he went to Colonel Jacob Ruppert and Ed Barrow and expressed an interest in managing the Yankees. But he encountered a stone wall and the job went to ex-Yankee pitcher Bob Shawkey. "How can you manage the Yankees," Ruppert asked him, perhaps rhetorically, "when you can't even manage yourself?"

Shawkey didn't last long, though; the 1930 season had barely ended before he was abruptly fired and replaced by Joe McCarthy, who had just been let go as manager of the Chicago Cubs. Ruth bitterly resented McCarthy from the start. In the Babe's opinion, he himself was much more qualified to manage the Yankees than McCarthy—a nonentity, in Ruth's eyes, who was never good enough to make it in the majors as a player.

McCarthy, needless to say, didn't like Ruth any more than Ruth liked him. Ruth was too swashbuckling, too boisterous for the conservative McCarthy. Perhaps even more important, the Babe represented an established power center on the Yankees, someone who could conceivably undermine McCarthy's authority.

The two coexisted because they had no alternative, but neither ever changed his mind about the other. Ruth regularly complained publicly about McCarthy's poor handling of the team and just as regularly suggested that a replacement—by the name of Babe Ruth—would be a distinct improvement. The two made sure they had no contact off the field, nor did their wives speak to each other. Matters came to a head on one occasion and McCarthy offered to resign, but Ruppert and Barrow refused to listen.

Ruth took a pay cut in 1933, despite his heroics in the 1932 World Series. He dropped from $75,000 all the way to $52,000. He was sliding down the same ladder he had climbed up a decade earlier. The fact that the country was in the throes of a crippling depression, with a quarter of the civilian labor force out of work, didn't strengthen the Babe's bargaining position. In 1934 Ruth signed his final Yankee contract—for $35,000. It was $45,000 below his $80,000 peak, but he was *still* the highest-paid player in the big leagues.

He hit only .301 in 1933 and just .288 in 1934. The Babe was approaching forty; he was no longer an offensive powerhouse and he was becoming a defensive liability. Even so, he hit 34 home runs in 1933 and 22 more (including number 700) in 1934, his twentieth full year in the majors. But he rarely played a complete game anymore. In late innings, McCarthy would replace him with Myril Hoag or Sammy Byrd—"Babe Ruth's legs," as the two of them were called.

Nevertheless, he closed the 1933 season with a razzle-dazzle performance at Yankee Stadium. In order to hype attendance, Barrow arranged for Ruth to pitch the last game of the year. He pitched the whole game and won, with the margin of victory being his own home run! "I had such a sore arm after pitching nine innings," he said "that I had to eat with my right hand for a week."

His skills might have been fading, but his popularity wasn't. After the 1933 season he played some exhibition games in Hawaii and in 1934 he played seventeen postseason games in Japan. In both places he was met by huge and enthusiastic crowds—an estimated half a million excited people turned out to welcome him in Tokyo, where he had never before set foot in his life.

And he was still the favorite of the *crème de la crème* of Park Avenue society, which had always been as fascinated by the Bambino as the shirt-sleeved fans in the bleachers. His personal magnetism cut across all class and social lines. There are many stories of his misadventures with the Social Register crowd, most of which fall into the "bull in the china shop" category.

A typical one, for example, concerns the time Christy Walsh took him to a formal dinner party where the matronly hostess, seated at the head of the table, inquired whether she might pass him the creamed asparagus.

"No, thank you," said the Babe, in his most polite and gracious manner, "it looks delicious but I never eat asparagus. It makes my urine smell."

Later, Walsh chided his companion: "Babe, you should watch your language. About the asparagus, that wasn't the proper thing to say."

Ruth was taken aback: "Jeez, whaddaya want, Christy? I was pretty proud of myself. I said *urine*, didn't I?"

The Babe's social graces were hampered by the fact that he never remembered anyone's name. Obviously, he could have recalled names if he'd wanted to, but he met so many people he decided, probably wisely, to forget the whole thing. The ultimate in forgetfulness occurred when pitcher Waite Hoyt was traded from the Yankees to Detroit in May of 1930, after the two of them had been teammates for a decade and close friends for most of that time.

"I hate to see you go," the Babe said, shaking hands in the clubhouse. "Now, you take care of yourself . . . er . . . Walter."

He called all males under the age of forty "Kid" (pronounced "Keed"). Once some gray hair appeared, they became "Doc" or "Pop." Younger women were "Sister" and older ones "Mom."

After Ruth hit his 58th home run in 1927, a man came into the clubhouse and asked the Babe if he would autograph a baseball. "I bought the ball off a kid," the man said. "It's the one you hit out of the park."

Ruth signed the ball and the visitor thanked him and left. "I wonder who that guy was," said the Babe, thinking out loud. "I'm pretty sure I've seen him someplace."

"You sure have," said third baseman Joe Dugan. "That was Hod Lisenbee, the pitcher who threw you that home run ball today."

On February 20, 1935, Babe and Claire returned from Japan via Paris and London. They had hardly gotten settled before they learned what they had both known deep down all along: that his days as a Yankee were coming to an end. His managerial ambitions had become a source of embarrassment to Ruppert and Barrow. They had no intention of replacing Joe McCarthy with anyone, much less Babe Ruth, and his continued sniping at McCarthy annoyed them.

For his part, Ruth announced that his playing days were over. He now wanted to be a manager. He was forty years old and had a lifetime total of 708 major league home runs to his credit, not counting another 15 in World Series competition. No one else was even close: Lou Gehrig was runner-up with 348, less than half Ruth's total, and Rogers Hornsby was next with 300. Everyone agreed that this was one record that would never be broken—no one would ever again come anywhere close to hitting the astonishing number of 700 home runs. (Henry Louis Aaron was a toddler in Mobile, Alabama—he had just turned one year old on February 5, 1935. Not that it mattered; blacks hadn't been allowed in major league baseball since the 1880s.)

Ruth did have several managing opportunities, but for one reason or another they all fell through. The Detroit Tigers had been interested in him late in 1933, but eventually they had turned to Mickey Cochrane instead. Ruth himself was largely to blame. Frank Navin, owner of the Tigers, asked him to come to Detroit to discuss the matter, but the Babe was on a tight exhibition game schedule and postponed the meeting. By the time Ruth was ready to meet, Navin had decided to hire Cochrane.

Not going to see Navin immediately was "one of the great boners of my career," Ruth wrote in his autobiography.

Yankee owner Colonel Ruppert suggested that Ruth manage the Newark Bears, a Yankee farm team in the International League, and learn how to manage in the minor leagues before taking on the responsibility of a big league team.

Ruth protested that Ty Cobb, Mickey Cochrane, Joe Cronin, Charlie Grimm, Bucky Harris, Rogers Hornsby, Christy Mathewson, John McGraw, Tris Speaker, and Bill Terry, to mention just a few, had all been made major league managers without an apprenticeship in the minors. Why not him? He had been a pitcher, an outfielder, occasionally a first baseman, and had been playing the game for twenty years. He was acknowledged as the greatest hitter in the game's history and had also been one of the best pitchers in the majors at one time. What additional qualifications did he need?

Claire encouraged him to turn down the Newark job. "Babe, you're a big leaguer," she said. "You've been in the big leagues all your life. That's where you belong."

In retrospect, it was probably a mistake to turn down the opportunity to manage Newark. Chances are Ruth would have done well because he would have had top-notch talent. The Yankees had a productive farm system in the 1930s and they stocked the Newark Bears with their best prospects. The Bears finished first in the International League in 1932, '33, and '34, and again in '37 and '38. Only one successful season in Newark would have been sufficient to catapult the Babe into a big league manager's role.

As matters then stood with respect to the majors, though, it always came down to the same old chestnut: "How can he manage others when he can't even manage himself?"

In fairness to Ruth, he was not the same person in the thirties that he had been in the twenties. Since he'd married Claire, he'd matured and managed himself quite well, certainly as well as most people. If all big league managers had to pass close inspections of their private lives, there would be a lot of rudderless ball clubs floundering around.

Whether the Babe would have made a good manager is an open question, because we never had a chance to find out. Great players rarely make good managers. Great *natural* players, like Ruth, often fail as managers because they get impatient when dealing with men whose natural talents are inferior to their own. The great ones who don't have overwhelming natural ability invariably have a compulsive drive to succeed that few others share; they tend to get upset because they think their players aren't trying hard enough.

On the other hand, Frank Chance, Mickey Cochrane, John McGraw, and Bill Terry were all outstanding players and successful managers as well.

In any event, it is an old baseball adage that a team makes a manager, a manager doesn't make a team. Given good material, Ruth would probably have been a decent manager; with poor material, he would probably, like everyone else, have gotten fired. Under Joe McCarthy, the New York Yankees finished second three years in a row and then won pennants in 1936, '37, '38, and '39. Chances are that even someone who couldn't manage himself could manage to win a few pennants with personnel like Lou Gehrig, Joe DiMaggio, Bill Dickey, Tommy Henrich, Lefty Gomez, and Red Ruffing.

The Boston Braves, a sick franchise, needed help, and in late February of 1935 Ruth was flimflammed into supplying it. Judge Emil Fuchs, owner of the Braves, offered Ruth a salary of $35,000 and the positions of vice-president, assistant manager, *and* active player (the Babe was going to have to earn every cent of that money). Dangled in front of his nose, although never promised explicitly, was the possibility that in the following year—1936—Ruth would succeed Bill McKechnie as the Braves' manager.

Many of Ruth's close friends advised him to turn down the Boston proposal. They felt he was being hustled and that there was little chance of his actually becoming manager of the Braves in 1936. They advised him to stay put, or to take the Newark job, instead of getting involved in an arrangement wherein the Braves would simply be exploiting his box-office value.

Unfortunately, anxiety, impatience, and wishful thinking overwhelmed Babe's better judgment, so that the 1935 season opened with Babe Ruth back in Boston but in a National League uniform. In a month or two he realized he had made a mistake. "Vice-president" and "assistant manager" turned out to be empty titles, carrying no duties or responsibilities. It also became clear that there was no real intention of appointing him manager in 1936.

Furthermore, he could no longer play well. He wanted to sit on the bench and manage, not play, but reluctantly agreed to take his place in the lineup because it was a condition of becoming "assistant manager" in 1935 and, he hoped, manager the next year.

The 1935 season opened on April 16—the New York Giants versus the

Boston Braves in Boston. Rising to the occasion once more, Ruth singled and homered off the great Carl Hubbell, driving in three runs in a 4–2 Boston victory.

Thereafter, however, everything went downhill except for one electrifying May afternoon in Pittsburgh. He hit a few more home runs, struck out a lot, but mostly stayed on the sidelines with assorted aches and pains, no longer able to drag himself all the way to the outfield on a daily basis. Baseball wasn't fun anymore—for the first time in his life, baseball had become drudgery and hard work.

Elbie Fletcher was a rookie first baseman with the Braves that year. "We were all awed by his presence," he recalled in the 1970s. "He still had that marvelous swing, and what a beautiful follow-through. But he was forty years old. He couldn't run, he could hardly bend down for a ball, and of course he couldn't hit the way he used to. It was sad watching those great skills fading away. To see it happening to Babe Ruth, to see Babe Ruth struggling on a ball field, well, that's when you realize we're all mortal and nothing lasts forever."

But there was that one glorious day in Pittsburgh's Forbes Field that almost made it all worthwhile. It was May 25, 1935, and Pittsburgh's starting pitcher was Red Lucas. Ruth came to bat with a man on base in the first inning and promptly drove a pitch into the right field seats.

When he came up again, Red Lucas had been replaced by Guy Bush—the same Guy Bush who with the Chicago Cubs had been Ruth's roughest heckler in the 1932 World Series. Again there was one man on, and again Ruth hammered the ball into the right field stands.

The third time up, he singled another run across the plate.

He came up for the fourth time in the seventh inning. Bush was still pitching for Pittsburgh. The bases were empty. With the count three balls and one strike, he got his entire body behind his next swing and lofted the ball high *over* the right field roof. According to the Associated Press account of the game, "It was a prodigious clout that carried clear over the right-field grandstand, bounded into the street, and rolled into Schenley Park. Baseball men said it was the longest drive ever hit at Forbes Field."

Thus did Babe Ruth hit his 714th home run. It was only the second time he had hit three home runs in a game in the regular season, although he had done so twice in World Series play. Although he didn't realize it then, this was the last time in a major league game that he would circle the bases with his short, mincing pigeon-toed steps in his famous home run trot. It was also his last big league hit.

Attendance was only 10,000 that day. Nevertheless, Ruth trotted around the bases for the third time to a thunderous ovation—although many older fans seemed to be crying as much as cheering.

Almost four decades later, pitcher Guy Bush remembered that moment: "I don't recall the first home run he hit off me that day. But I'll never forget the second one. He got hold of that ball and hit it clear out of the ballpark. It was the longest cockeyed ball I ever saw in my life. That poor fellow, he'd gotten to where he could hardly hobble along. When he rounded third base, I looked over there at him and he kind of looked at me. I tipped my cap, sort of to say, 'I've seen everything now, Babe.' He looked at me and kind of saluted and smiled. We got in that gesture of good friendship. And that's the last home run he ever hit."

Getting in shape for the 1933 season at Artie McGovern's gymnasium, with Julia's help. Artie himself, almost hidden, is the referee.

Colonel Ruppert and the Babe, for once without a contract in front of them.

On Sunday, October 1, 1933, the last day of the season, a crowd of 25,000 showed up at the Stadium to see Babe Ruth pitch once again. The Yankees had already been mathematically eliminated from the pennant race. Ruth hurled all nine innings, belted a home run in the fifth, and beat the Red Sox, 6–5.

Here Boston outfielder Smead Jolley is at bat as Ruth pitches. The catcher is Joe Glenn, the shortstop is Frank Crosetti, and the infield umpire is George Moriarty.

Frank J. Navin, president of the Detroit Tigers from 1908 until his death in 1935. In October of 1933 he was prepared to make Babe Detroit's manager, but Ruth postponed a meeting for so long that Navin became annoyed and changed his mind. Mickey Cochrane got the job and promptly won two pennants in a row.

The Babe is presenting a scroll to pitcher Carl Hubbell, who has been named to Christy Walsh's 1933 All-American team. In the second All-Star Game, played in 1934, Hubbell struck out Babe Ruth, Lou Gehrig, Jimmie Foxx, Al Simmons, and Joe Cronin in succession. (In the first All-Star Game, in 1933, Babe Ruth — who else? — had hit the first All-Star homer.)

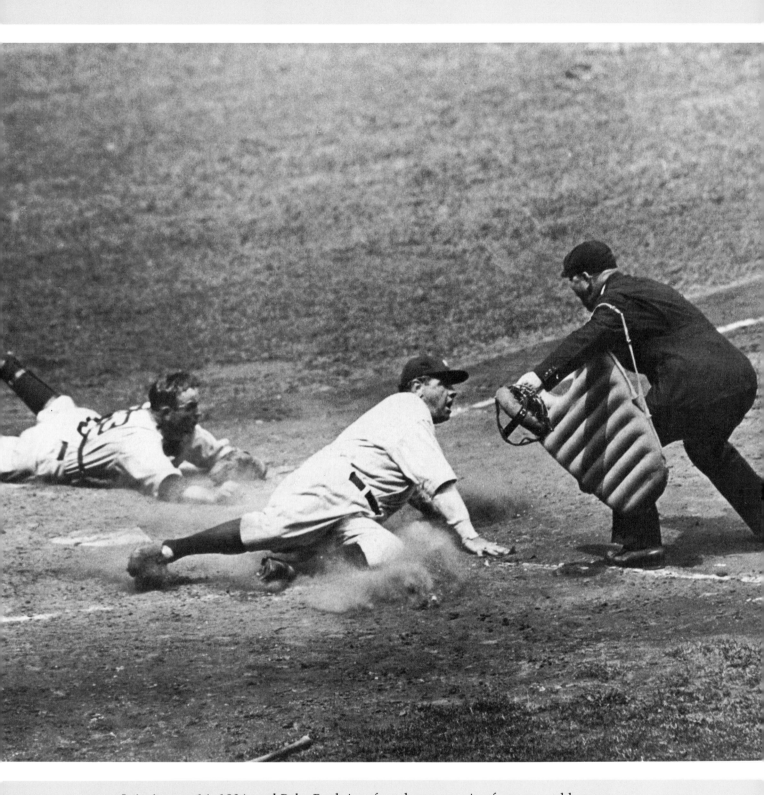

It is August 14, 1934, and Babe Ruth is safe at home, scoring from second base on a single by Bill Dickey. The catcher is Detroit's Ray Hayworth and the umpire is Lou Kolls.

LEFT: Babe Ruth has just played his last game as a New York Yankee. The date is September 30, 1934.

BELOW: It is still September 30, and Ruth is leaving the ballpark after the game.

LEFT: In November of 1934 Ruth and a team of big leaguers visited Japan to play a series of exhibition games. A caricature of his face was enough of a symbol to publicize the tour.

BELOW: In Tokyo the Japanese went delirious with joy at seeing Beibu Rusu. Half a million people greeted him on his arrival.

Wherever they went in Japan, the easily recognizable American ballplayers drew a small army of followers. Below, an audience of one can sometimes be as satisfying as an audience of thousands.

Ruth at bat in a game in Tokyo.

With Japanese batboys in Osaka. The people are the same above and below but there's been a hat switch.

ABOVE: The old hat switch! They always love it. The Babe didn't dream it up as a brand-new idea in Osaka. Here his is in the Philadelphia A's dugout just prior to the third game of the 1931 World Series, A's vs. Cardinals. The man wearing Babe's cap is Philadelphia catcher Mickey Cochrane. (See also the photo taken in Sharon, Pennsylvania, on page 123.)

RIGHT: The face is familiar but the uniform isn't. It is March of 1935 and Babe Ruth is now at spring training as a Boston Brave.

RIGHT: Judge Emil Edwin
Fuchs, owner of the Boston
Braves from 1923 to August of
1935. In 1929 he made himself
manager, but the team still
finished last.

BELOW: The routine isn't so
different, after all.

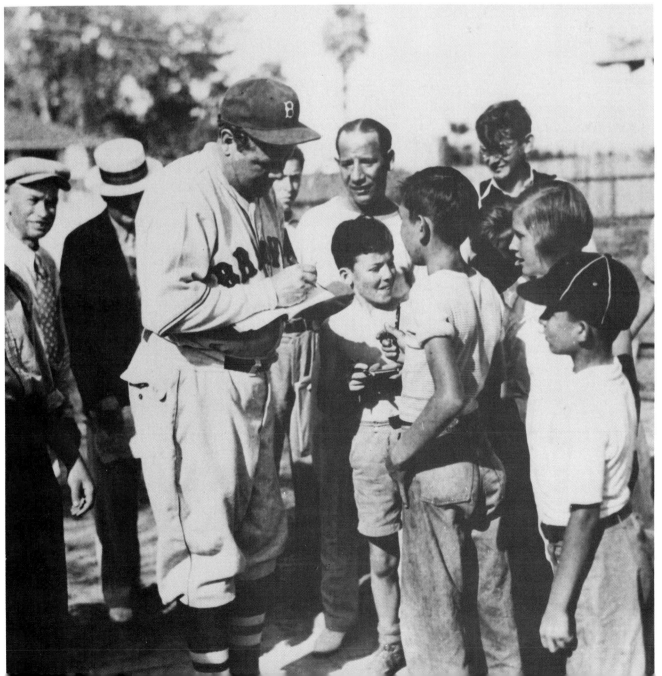

Veteran shortstop Rabbit Maranville, five feet five inches tall and three years *older* than Ruth, was also at spring training with the Braves in '35. They kept each other company.

ABOVE: Former heavyweight wrestling champion Ed "Strangler" Lewis shows the Babe how he used to do it.

RIGHT: With Braves home run slugger Wally Berger, who had hit 38 round-trippers in 1930, his rookie season.

Claire Ruth in 1935 at the age of thirty-five.

BELOW: With Braves Manager Bill McKechnie and young Jimmy McKechnie, Bill's son. The rumor was that Ruth would replace McKechnie as manager of the Braves in 1936, but of course it never came to pass.

Don't fence me in. Yankee Manager Joe McCarthy and Boston Manager Bill McKechnie
have the Babe hemmed in, in more ways than one, and his feelings aren't hard to decipher.

ABOVE: It is April 21, 1935, and Ruth has just homered off pitcher Ray Benge of the Brooklyn Dodgers at Braves Field. The catcher is Al Lopez, the on-deck batter Wally Berger, and the home plate umpire is Dolly Stark. Also visible are Bill McKechnie (number 33) as third base coach and third base umpire Charlie Rigler. It is Ruth's 710th career homer, and he will hit just four more before he retires on June 2.

RIGHT: Pitcher Guy Bush, another tough cookie. On the Chicago Cubs in 1932, he had been the loudest and most obnoxious of Ruth's hecklers during the '32 World Series. Subsequently traded to Pittsburgh, he gave up Ruth's 713th and 714th home runs on May 25, 1935 — the day the Babe had his last glorious hurrah.

As Ruth rounded the bases for his third home run of the day — the last he would ever hit in the big leagues — Bush made the extraordinary gesture of tipping his cap as a sign of admiration.

It is May 25, 1935, Forbes Field, Boston vs. Pittsburgh, third inning, and George Herman Ruth has just hit his second homer of the game, the 713th of his career. Ruth is approaching home plate, with Boston second baseman Les Mallon scoring ahead of him. Bill McKechnie is Boston's third base coach and Wally Berger is the on-deck batter. Pittsburgh catcher Earl Grace is at the pitching mound, talking things over with Guy Bush. Tommy Thevenow is the Pirates' third baseman. The home plate umpire is Beans Reardon and the third base umpire is Charlie Moran.

Of Babe Ruth's 714 lifetime home runs, 347 were hit at home and 367 on the road; 499 were hit against right-handed pitchers and 215 against lefties.

GEORGE HERMAN (BABE) RUTH

233

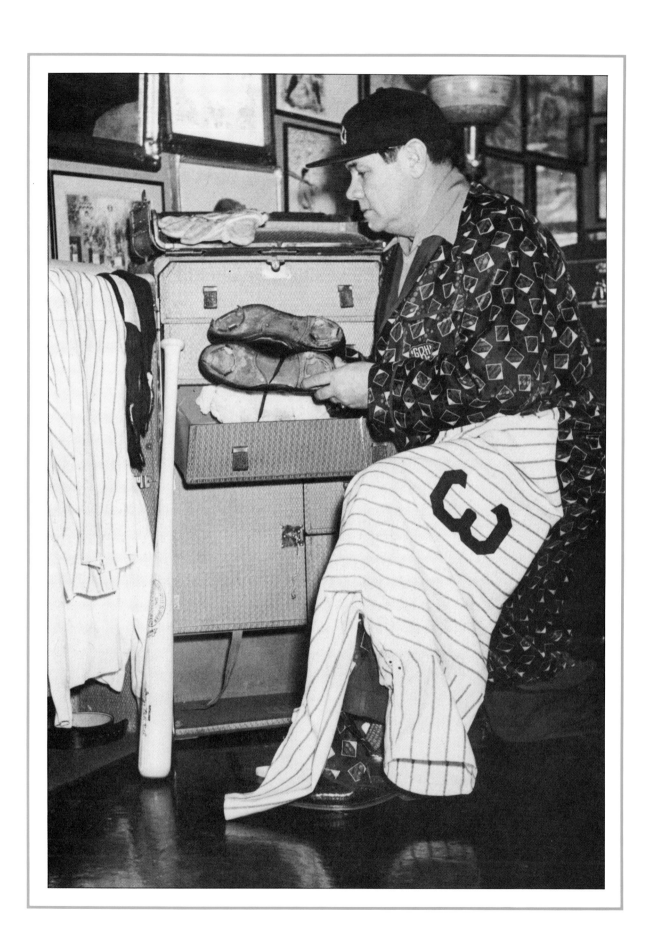

Final Innings
1935-1948

It is a widely held misconception that Babe Ruth hit three home runs in his last major league game. The misconception is understandable because at the time everyone agreed he *should* retire after hitting those three dramatic homers in Pittsburgh on May 25, 1935. Everyone agreed, that is, except the Babe. He hung on for another week or so, hoping against hope that the old magic was back.

But of course it wasn't. On May 26 he got no hits and fanned three times. On the twenty-seventh he came up only as a pinch hitter and walked. Nor did he get a hit on the twenty-eighth or twenty-ninth. He played in his last major league game on May 30: he grounded out in the first inning and then benched himself.

Three days later, on June 2 in Boston, he announced his retirement as an active player. Braves' owner Emil Fuchs fired him on the same day. Not that it matters, but just for the record no one knows whether he quit before he got fired or got fired before he quit.

Angry and frustrated, Babe and Claire promptly drove home from Boston. In Claire's words, "From then until the day he died, Babe Ruth, figuratively, sat by the telephone" waiting for a call to manage in the major leagues, waiting for a call that never came.

Aside from sitting by the phone, what did he do with himself now that he was out of baseball? He played a lot of golf, bowled regularly, went hunting and fishing occasionally, had his own radio program from time to time, and made innumerable talks and personal appearances, often at hospitals and orphanages. In the evening he generally played cards with friends or listened to his favorite radio programs, especially "The Lone Ranger" and "Gangbusters." And he grew increasingly bitter that no one in baseball wanted him.

On February 2, 1936, Ruth was pleased to learn that he was one of five charter members elected to the brand-new Baseball Hall of Fame at Cooperstown. Of 226 ballots cast, Ty Cobb was named on 222, Ruth on 215, Honus Wagner on 215, Christy Mathewson on 205, and Walter Johnson on 189. No one else received the 170 votes that were needed for election.

With the passage of time, Ruth's star has risen relative to Cobb's. In 1969 Babe Ruth was voted "the greatest player of all time" by baseball writers and broadcasters celebrating the centennial of professional baseball, which began in 1869 with the Cincinnati Red Stockings.

In the middle of the 1938 season, the Brooklyn Dodgers hired him ostensibly as first base coach but really as a gate attraction. It didn't work out well, however, and he wasn't asked to return in 1939, when Leo Durocher became Brooklyn's manager. Ruth and Durocher had never gotten along, dating back to when they were teammates on the Yankees in the late twenties. (Durocher, by the way, got the Dodger job without any minor league managerial experience!)

Aside from Durocher, Ruth had other problems with the Dodgers. One day he saw a Brooklyn player roughly push an autograph-seeking youngster out of the way. "Here, kid," he said to the youngster, loud enough for the player to hear, "I'll sign for you."

He tried to be friendly, as always, but sometimes it backfired. On a road trip in August, Ruth was sitting in the club car when a young man sat down next to him. "I used to know every reporter who covered the New York teams," the Babe said, "but I don't know a lot of you young guys. What paper are you with?"

"I'm not with any newspaper," said the young man.

"What do you do, then?"

"I play left field for the Dodgers."

It was Tuck Stainback. Actually, it wasn't as bad as it sounds. Stainback was a newcomer to the Dodgers, having just joined the team a few weeks earlier.

Employed or not, Ruth had no money worries. Enough of his huge past earnings had been saved and invested wisely by Christy Walsh and Claire, so that the Ruths enjoyed a substantial lifetime income from trust funds. Soon after their wedding, Claire had instituted a household budget system that reinforced Christy Walsh's conservative financial management.

They agreed that she would be the only one allowed to write checks.

Anytime Babe wanted money, Claire would sign a fifty-dollar check for him; it would never be larger than fifty dollars, but she would write as many as he wished. "It was a tiring thing for both of us," she said, "but it served the purpose of cutting down on such Ruthian habits as tipping a hundred dollars for a thirty-five-cent ham sandwich."

On May 1, 1939, Yankee first baseman Lou Gehrig felt weak and uncoordinated and sat out a game for the first time since 1925, thus ending his streak of playing in 2,130 consecutive games. Doctors discovered that the thirty-five-year-old "Iron Man" was the victim of an incurable rare illness, amyotrophic lateral sclerosis, now called Lou Gehrig's disease.

A special Lou Gehrig Appreciation Day was held at Yankee Stadium on July the Fourth, with many of Gehrig's old Yankee teammates present. Ruth and Gehrig had been close friends for many years, but since 1934 they had gone their separate ways.

The events behind the rupture sound trivial, but they were important to those involved. Apparently, Lou Gehrig's mother criticized the clothes worn by young Dorothy Ruth. Mom Gehrig implied that Claire Ruth took better care of Julia, her natural daughter, than she did of Dorothy, her adopted daughter. These remarks infuriated Claire, and it wasn't long before the Babe was angry as well. The big fellow thereupon let Lou know, in no uncertain terms, that he thought Mom Gehrig (a) had a big mouth, (b) should mind her own business, and (c) didn't know what she was talking about in the first place.

The Iron Horse could take a lot of punishment, but the one thing he couldn't take was criticism of his mother. Thereafter, the two Yankee sluggers spoke to each other on the field only when necessary and off the field not at all.

They made up on that sad July the Fourth, however. Standing in the infield, surrounded by old teammates and 70,000 silent fans, Lou delivered a speech that Gary Cooper would make famous in *The Pride of the Yankees* ("Today I consider myself the luckiest man on the face of the earth"). Afterward Babe rushed over and embraced him.

"I put my arms around him," Ruth said, "and though I tried to smile and cheer him up, I wound up crying like a baby."

Gehrig died less than two years later, shortly before his thirty-eighth birthday. For someone with ALS, his illness was mercifully brief.

Babe Ruth couldn't know it as he stood hugging Lou Gehrig, but in a surprisingly short while he would find himself in the same spot, standing in the same infield, a death sentence also passed, also saying good-bye. The greatest one-two punch in baseball history—only this time, for the first time, Gehrig preceded Ruth.

With the outbreak of World War II, Ruth was wheeled around like a

Living Monument to sell War Bonds and raise money for the war effort. He was only forty-six years old, close to forty-seven, when the Japanese bombed Pearl Harbor, but he'd already been in the public spotlight for over a quarter of a century. He did whatever was asked of him, always happy to be of use. He even developed into a skillful fund-raiser: he'd always had an abundance of charisma and by now he'd become an experienced public speaker as well.

The Babe's effectiveness in selling War Bonds was enormously enhanced when it was reported that Japanese infantrymen charging American trenches in the Pacific were shouting, "To hell with Babe Ruth!" (in English, naturally).

On August 23, 1942, the Yankees put on a special show with part of the admissions going to the Army-Navy Relief Fund: a crowd of over 69,000 showed up at Yankee Stadium to see Walter Johnson pitch to Babe Ruth between games of a Sunday afternoon doubleheader. Johnson threw twenty-one pitches. Ruth hit the third into the lower right field stands and the last high into the third deck in right, a tremendous shot. It landed a few feet foul, but Babe didn't let that bother him; he simply went into his familiar home run trot, smiling and tipping his cap and basking in thunderous applause all the way around the bases.

After touching home plate, Ruth kept on going right into the dugout on the way to the locker room, along with Walter Johnson, but the applause continued undiminished for many minutes after they had both disappeared. "People think they're cheering for Babe Ruth and Walter Johnson to return and take a bow," remarked a sportswriter, "but what they're really doing is trying to bring back their own lost youth."

In the fall of 1946, the Babe started to get severe pains over his left eye. His voice also began to get hoarse. The pain became so bad that on November 26 he entered French Hospital on West Thirtieth Street. Doctors discovered he had throat cancer, although they never told him in so many words.

Surgeons operated and did what they could: "They dug into my neck and tied up the nerves that were transmitting pain to my eye and jaw and head in general. When they could move me, they wheeled me back in front of the X-ray machines and gave me so many treatments that my hair came out in hunks when the nurses tried to comb it. I lost 80 pounds and there were times when I felt I would die."

The Babe left French Hospital on February 15, 1947. He'd been there almost three months. He was too frail to walk a short distance to his car without help.

With the end obviously near, April 27, a Sunday, was declared Babe

Ruth Day in every ballpark in organized baseball in the United States as well as in Japan. Ruth was not up to putting on his old Yankee uniform, but he made an appearance at the Stadium in sports clothes and his familiar camel's-hair coat and cap. As he was being driven to the ballpark, and helped onto the field, he must have thought more than once about Lou Gehrig. It was only eight years before that he had embraced his old friend at Yankee Stadium under circumstances depressingly similar.

His voice over the loudspeakers, after the operation, was a hoarse whisper, terrible in its intimation of impending death: "You know how bad my voice sounds," he said. "Well, it feels just as bad."

He spoke briefly, with obvious effort. "There have been so many lovely things said about me today," he concluded, "that I am glad to have had the opportunity to thank everybody. Thank you."

Before his operation, Ruth had a pleasing baritone voice. As a frame of reference, his voice sounded a lot like Clark Gable's. Now it was a pitiful croak, a hoarse whisper that only got worse over the remaining year and a half of his lifetime.

Why did he get throat cancer?

The use of tobacco cannot be ignored as a possible cause. Babe was chewing and smoking tobacco by the age of seven, and he remained a heavy smoker all his life. He also used so much snuff it eventually clogged his nasal passages, so that doctors ordered him to stop. He smoked cigarettes and a pipe when he was in his teens and twenties, but as he grew older he preferred cigars, smoking a dozen or more a day. (Notice the number of photographs in which he has a cigar in his mouth or is holding one in his hand.)

Against all odds, he held on for another year and a half. His final appearance at Yankee Stadium came on June 13, 1948, when the Yankees celebrated the twenty-fifth anniversary of the House That Ruth Built and took the occasion to retire his famous uniform number 3. For that reason, he put the uniform on once more, the last time it would ever be worn.

The Yankees invited many of his former teammates to be on hand for the ceremonies. Most of them were already in the locker room, milling around and exchanging greetings, when he arrived. "Here he is now," someone said softly, as the door opened and he entered the room, assisted by friends on each side. His old teammates came over to shake hands, touch him, put their arms around him, straining to hear his gravelly whispers. They helped him get into his uniform, and then he waited in the locker room as they went out onto the field to be introduced. He was chilly, so a topcoat was put over his shoulders.

After what seemed to be a long time, he was led from the locker room to the dugout. Finally, when everyone else had been introduced and there was only one left, he took his bat in hand. As Mel Allen announced his name—"George Herman Ruth . . . Babe Ruth!"—and it echoed and reechoed over the Stadium's public address system, he rose to his feet, let the topcoat slide off his shoulders, and, in the words of W. C. Heinz, "walked out into the cauldron of sound he must have known better than any other man."

A few moments later he was the subject of what has been called "one of sport's most poignant photos": photographed from the back, cap in hand, head slightly bowed, thin and frail, Ruth is facing toward the right field seats, where so many of his mighty home runs had landed—only now the bat that was such a lethal weapon has become a cane that he leans on for support.

Time was almost up.

On July 26 he went into the hospital—Memorial Hospital, on East Sixty-eighth Street. From then on, his wife, Claire, sister, Mamie, and daughters, Dorothy and Julia, were with him constantly. He died at 8:01 P.M. on August 16, 1948. He was only fifty-three and a half years old.

His body lay in state on August 17 and 18 in a mahogany coffin placed in the main entrance of Yankee Stadium. He was dressed in a simple blue double-breasted suit, a set of black rosary beads wrapped about his left hand. Estimates of the number of people who filed by his bier to pay their last respects range from a hundred thousand to a quarter of a million. They stood in line for hours, all ages and social classes, many of them fathers who lifted up their children as they passed the coffin so the youngsters could catch a glimpse of Babe Ruth.

The funeral was held on August 19 in New York's St. Patrick's Cathedral. Tens of thousands massed in the streets around the cathedral before the requiem mass was scheduled to begin and stood silently while it was in progress. The route the funeral cortege took to the cemetery was similarly lined with unnumbered thousands who waited hours to see it pass.

In the twentieth century, only the deaths of Franklin Delano Roosevelt and John Fitzgerald Kennedy have evoked such deep and pervasive sorrow from the American people. His passing touched an emotional chord that was felt throughout the length and breadth of the land.

Among the pallbearers on that muggy August day were Joe Dugan and Waite Hoyt, Ruth's old Yankee teammates. "I'd give a hundred bucks for an ice-cold beer," Dugan whispered, sweating under the burden of the coffin.

"So would the Babe," Hoyt whispered back.

Indeed, it was the same Waite Hoyt who unwittingly uttered the most fitting epitaph of all for George Herman Ruth: "God, we liked that big son of a bitch," said Hoyt. "He was a constant source of joy."

Babe Ruth is buried at Gate of Heaven Cemetery in Hawthorne, New York, twenty-five miles north of Yankee Stadium. Claire Ruth lived at 110 Riverside Drive for another twenty-eight years. She died on October 25, 1976, at the age of seventy-six. She is buried beside her husband.

It is June 3, 1935, a day after Babe Ruth has quit the Boston Braves (or been fired — it was never clear which). He is saying good-bye to Manager Bill McKechnie as he and Claire prepare to drive home from Boston. In the privacy of the car, he cried most of the way home.

BELOW: Babe has just arrived home in New York, where he is met by a surprise welcome-home crowd from the neighborhood.

What to do? According to Claire: "From then until the day he died, Babe Ruth, figuratively, sat by the telephone" waiting for a call to manage in the major leagues, waiting for a call that never came.

Golf became a major preoccupation in his first years after baseball. Indeed, for a while he even toyed with the idea of becoming a professional. Although he was a very good amateur golfer, most of those in a position to know thought he was a notch below professional standards.

Every once in a while, but less and less often, Babe and Claire would take in a game at Yankee Stadium. It is said that he phoned for tickets for Opening Day one year and was told he'd have to send a check for the appropriate amount first.

LEFT: On the Detroit Tigers' bench before the last game of the 1935 World Series (which Detroit won). On the right is Detroit third base coach Del Baker.

BELOW: Of course, there were always baseballs to sign—more than ever, it seemed.

Babe still loved to hunt. Claire didn't, but sometimes she went along anyway just to keep him company.

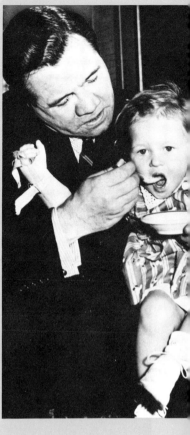

Unfailingly, he was available for the kids, especially in hospitals. When it came to children, Babe had always given more love than he'd received. Now the balance was shifting.

Early in 1936. Left to right: Julia, Babe, Claire (at the piano), and Dorothy.

A chilly fall afternoon. The baseball season is over. A playing career is over.
What could be going through his mind?

A new book, *Babe Ruth's Baseball Advice*, made its appearance, and Giant outfielder Mel Ott looks interested. But no one else seemed to much care about Babe Ruth's baseball advice.

Joe DiMaggio's first year in Yankee pinstripes was 1936. Here DiMaggio and Ruth meet at the New York Baseball Writers' Dinner in January 1937. Sportswriter Bill Corum is in the center.

In mid-1938 Larry MacPhail, executive vice-president of the Brooklyn Dodgers, asked Ruth to become Brooklyn's first base coach. It was implied he might become manager next year. He joined the team on June 19, weighing at least 250 pounds, a good 30 pounds overweight.

Dorothy (left) and Claire came over to Brooklyn to see how he was doing. Apparently no one in the Ruth household was going hungry.

With "Poosh 'Em Up" Tony Lazzeri, now a second stringer with the Chicago Cubs. Ruth and Lazzeri had been teammates on the Yankees from '26 through '34 and had also been close friends off the field.

The Dodgers wound up next to last in 1938, but one might say that the season ended on a high note anyway. Left to right: outfielders Tuck Stainback, Buddy Hassett, Kiki Cuyler, and the first base coach.

BELOW: (Left to right:) Manager Burleigh Grimes, Ruth, and shortstop Leo Durocher in the summer of 1938. It was not Ruth but Durocher who became the Dodgers' manager in 1939. This meant "Exit for Mr. Ruth." They had been teammates long ago and had never liked one another. According to Claire: "It was the Babe's feeling that deft shortstop play was the sum total of Leo's civilized conduct."

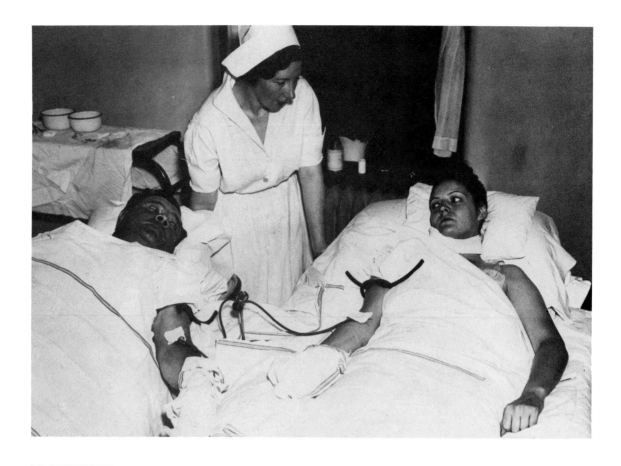

ABOVE: In August, Ruth was rushed from a Dodger game to Julia's bedside. She had become ill and needed a blood transfusion. Fortunately his was the appropriate blood type and he was able to supply whatever was necessary.

Everything turned out all right: it is three years later and the Babe is walking down the aisle to give away his daughter Julia in marriage.

Still a photographer's
dream. You name it,
he'll do it.

July 4, 1939, Lou Gehrig Appreciation Day at Yankee Stadium: "Today I consider myself the luckiest man on the face of the earth." Henry Louis Gehrig was born June 19, 1903. He died on June 2, 1941, of the disease that bears his name.

Filming *The Pride of the Yankees*, starring Gary Cooper as Lou Gehrig. In a previous take of this scene, representing a celebration of Yankee players after a World Series victory, Babe accidentally cut his hand by exuberantly punching it through a train window. (Big league clubs didn't begin to travel by plane until the late forties.) The Babe attacks the scene in no-holds-barred fashion as he pulls a straw hat over a teammate's head as part of the celebration.

On August 23, 1942, at Yankee Stadium, the great Walter Johnson will pitch once more to Babe Ruth, this time in an exhibition for the benefit of Army–Navy Relief. Above, the Babe is coming to the Stadium a few days prior to the event to take batting practice.

It is August 23 and the exhibition is scheduled for between games of today's New York–Washington double header. In anticipation of seeing Johnson and Ruth once again, 69,000 fans have jammed the ballpark. Here, the two veterans are under the stands waiting (eagerly? anxiously? apprehensively?) to be called onto the field.

Johnson pitching, Ruth batting, once again. Walter threw twenty-one pitches and Babe managed to hit two of them into the stands—he hit the third pitch into the lower right field stands and the last one high up into the top deck in right. The catcher was Ruth's old teammate and buddy Benny Bengough, and the umpire is Billy Evans.

At about the same time, Ruth and Ty Cobb—never the greatest of friends—
hooked up for a series of benefit golf matches. Like John McGraw, Ty Cobb had
always ridiculed Ruth's homer-happy style of game. McGraw and Cobb had been
the leading practitioners of one-run-at-a-time "strategy" baseball. Ruth had
revolutionized the national pastime, and the king he had dethroned was Tyrus
Raymond Cobb. But all that was in the past, and by now the two could coexist
tolerably well.

In 1944 Babe had to go to the hospital for the removal of painful cartilage from his knee. Here he inspects the offending tissue the surgeons have removed.

With Claire in Florida in March of 1947. In January, Babe had undergone major surgery at French Hospital in New York. The doctors found he had throat cancer and the prognosis was not good. He was still in the hospital on February 6, his fifty-second birthday. Soon thereafter he went to Florida with Claire and their dog, Pal, to recuperate.

April 27, 1947—Babe Ruth Day proclaimed in Yankee Stadium and in every ballpark in the United States and in Japan as well. The ceremonies were carried by radio to all other major league parks. "You know how bad my voice sounds," he said. "Well, it feels just as bad."

Behind Ruth, left to right: National League President Ford Frick, announcer Mel Allen, Francis Cardinal Spellman, and Commissioner Happy Chandler. At one time, Ford Frick, then a sportswriter, had been one of the Babe's ghost-writers.

A chat with Ted Williams before a Red Sox spring training game in March of 1948. It is still an open question which of the two was the greatest hitter in baseball history.

Showing William Bendix how to bat on the set of the movie *The Babe Ruth Story*. Bendix played the title role. The film was made in Hollywood in the spring of 1948. For once Gehrig topped Ruth, because *The Babe Ruth Story* turned out to be a piece of trash while *The Pride of the Yankees* remains one of the best sports movies ever made.

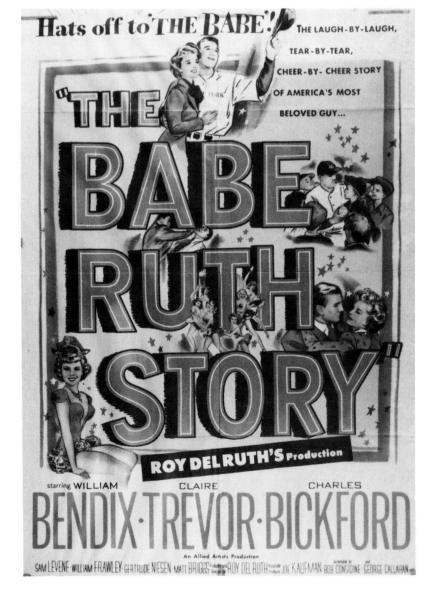

And still the children. Santa Claus for young polio victims at Christmastime 1947, and the Easter Seal campaign for crippled children in 1948 (the bat and ball are covered with Easter Seals).

In 1947, despite his failing health, Babe became a roving goodwill ambassador for American Legion Junior Baseball, a nationwide baseball program for youngsters. Here he extolls the program's benefits before a somewhat-less-than-overflow crowd at Fenway Park. "I won't be happy," he said, "until we have every boy in America between the ages of six and sixteen wearing a glove and swinging a bat."

LEFT: Babe is presenting the manuscript of his book *The Babe Ruth Story* to Yale University. The presentation is taking place on June 6, 1948, at a Yale-Princeton baseball game in New Haven, Connecticut. Accepting the gift is Yale captain and first baseman George Bush.

BELOW: Special ceremonies were held at Yankee Stadium on June 13, 1948, before a game with the Cleveland Indians, to mark the ballpark's Silver Anniversary (1923–1948). The Yankees used the occasion to permanently retire Babe Ruth's uniform number 3. It was, after all, the twenty-fifth anniversary of The House That Ruth Built.

Here Babe points out his old locker to former teammates and old friends Bob Meusel (left) and Mark Koenig.

The Silver Anniversary ceremonies featured the introduction of many former Yankees. After all the others had been announced and had lined up along the first base line, it was time to introduce the one everyone had come to see, had been waiting for since the beginning. He sat in the visiting team's dugout until he heard his name and then stepped for the last time onto the infield grass, bat in hand, into the "cauldron of sound he must have known better than any other man."

Perhaps the most famous
photograph in all of
sports history. It was
taken by Nat Fein for the
New York *Herald
Tribune* on June 13,
1948.

Yankee Stadium on the night of August 17, 1948. Babe Ruth died on August 16. He was only fifty-three and a half years old. His body lay in state on August 17 and 18 in a mahogany coffin placed in the main entrance of Yankee Stadium. The Stadium was kept open until midnight to accommodate the long lines of people who wanted to pay their last respects. Many waited in line for hours.

August 19. Part of the crowd on Fifth Avenue across from St. Patrick's Cathedral waiting to see the funeral cortege pass by. Honorary pallbearers were sportswriter Fred Lieb, Connie Mack of the Philadelphia Athletics, and former teammates Joe Dugan, Waite Hoyt, and Whitey Witt.

BABE RUTH'S RECORD

BATTING

YEAR	CLUB	LEAGUE	G	AB	SO	BB[1]	H	SB	2B	3B	R	HR	HR%[2]	AB/HR[3]	RBI	BA	SA[4]
1914	Balt.–Prov.	Int'l.	46	121	–	–	28	4	2	10	22	1	0.8	121.0	–	.231	.438
1914	Boston	Amer.	5	10	4	0	2	0	1	0	1	0	0.0	–	0	.200	.300
1915	Boston	Amer.	42	92	23	9	29	0	10	1	16	4	4.3	23.0	21	.315	.576
1916	Boston	Amer.	67	136	23	10	37	0	5	3	18	3	2.2	45.3	16	.272	.419
1917	Boston	Amer.	52	123	18	12	40	0	6	3	14	2	1.6	61.5	12	.325	.472
1918	Boston	Amer.	95	317	58*	57	95	6	26	11	50	11*	3.5*	28.8*	66	.300	.555*
1919	Boston	Amer.	130	432	58	101	139	7	34	12	103*	29*	6.7*	14.9*	114*	.322	.657*
1920	New York	Amer.	142	458	80	148*	172	14	36	9	158*	54*	11.8*	8.5*	137*	.376	.847*
1921	New York	Amer.	152	540	81	144*	204	17	44	16	177*	59*	10.9*	9.2*	171*	.378	.846*
1922	New York	Amer.	110	406	80	84	128	2	24	8	94	35	8.6*	11.5*	99	.315	.672*
1923	New York	Amer.	152	522	93*	170*	205	17	45	13	151*	41*	7.9*	12.7*	131*	.393	.764*
1924	New York	Amer.	153	529	81*	142*	200	9	39	7	143*	46*	8.7*	11.5*	121	.378*	.739*
1925	New York	Amer.	98	359	68	59	104	2	12	2	61	25	7.0	14.4	66	.290	.543
1926	New York	Amer.	152	495	76	144*	184	11	30	5	139*	47*	9.5*	10.5*	145*	.372	.737*
1927	New York	Amer.	151	540	89*	138*	192	7	29	8	158*	60*	11.1*	9.0*	164	.356	.772*
1928	New York	Amer.	154	536	87*	135*	173	4	29	8	163*	54*	10.1*	9.9*	142*	.323	.709*
1929	New York	Amer.	135	499	60	72	172	5	26	6	121	46*	9.2*	10.8*	154	.345	.697*
1930	New York	Amer.	145	518	61	136*	186	10	28	9	150	49*	9.5*	10.6*	153	.359	.732*
1931	New York	Amer.	145	534	51	128*	199	5	31	3	149	46*	8.6*	11.6*	163	.373	.700*
1932	New York	Amer.	133	457	62	130*	156	2	13	5	120	41	9.0	11.1	137	.341	.661
1933	New York	Amer.	137	459	90	114*	138	4	21	3	97	34	7.4	13.5	103	.301	.582
1934	New York	Amer.	125	365	63	103	105	1	17	4	78	22	6.0	16.6	84	.288	.537
1935	Boston	Nat'l.	28	72	24	20	13	0	0	0	13	6	8.3	12.0	12	.181	.431
MAJOR LEAGUE TOTALS			2,503	8,399	1,330	2,056	2,873	123	506	136	2,174	714	8.5	11.8	2,211	.342	.690

BATTING / WORLD SERIES

YEAR	CLUB	LEAGUE	G	AB	SO	BB	H	SB	2B	3B	R	HR	HR%	AB/HR	RBI	BA	SA
1915	Boston	Amer.	1	1	0	0	0	0	0	0	0	0	0.0	–	0	.000	.000
1916	Boston	Amer.	1	5	2	0	0	0	0	0	0	0	0.0	–	1	.000	.000
1918	Boston	Amer.	3	5	2	0	1	0	0	1	0	0	0.0	–	2	.200	.600
1921	New York	Amer.	6	16	8	5	5	2	0	0	3	1	6.3	16.0	4	.313	.500
1922	New York	Amer.	5	17	3	2	2	0	1	0	1	0	0.0	–	1	.118	.176
1923	New York	Amer.	6	19	6	8	7	0	1	1	8	3	15.8	6.3	3	.368	1.000
1926	New York	Amer.	7	20	2	11	6	1	0	0	6	4	20.0	5.0	5	.300	.900
1927	New York	Amer.	4	15	2	2	6	1	0	0	4	2	13.3	7.5	7	.400	.800
1928	New York	Amer.	4	16	2	1	10	0	3	0	9	3	18.8	5.3	4	.625	1.375
1932	New York	Amer.	4	15	3	4	5	0	0	0	6	2	13.3	7.5	6	.333	.733
WORLD SERIES TOTALS			41	129	30	33	42	4	5	2	37	15	11.6	8.6	33	.326	.744

THE BABE

BATTING / ALL-STAR GAMES

YEAR	LEAGUE	AB	SO	BB	H	SB	2B	3B	R	HR	HR%	AB/HR	RBI	BA	SA
1933	American	4	2	0	2	0	0	0	1	1	25.0	4.0	2	.500	1.250
1934	American	2	1	2	0	0	0	0	1	0	0.0	—	0	.000	.000
ALL-STAR TOTALS		6	3	2	2	0	0	0	2	1	16.7	6.0	2	.333	.833

PITCHING

YEAR	CLUB	LEAGUE	G	IP	W	L	PCT.	H	R	ER	SO	BB	ERA
1914	Balt.–Prov.	Int'l.	35	245	22	9	.710	219	88	—	139	101	—
1914	Boston	Amer.	4	23	2	1	.667	21	12	10	3	7	3.91
1915	Boston	Amer.	32	218	18	8	.692	166	80	59	112	85	2.44
1916	Boston	Amer.	44	324	23	12	.657	230	83	63	170	118	1.75*
1917	Boston	Amer.	41	326	24	13	.649	244	93	73	128	108	2.02
1918	Boston	Amer.	20	166	13	7	.650	125	51	41	40	49	2.22
1919	Boston	Amer.	17	133	9	5	.643	148	59	44	30	58	2.97
1920	New York	Amer.	1	4	1	0	1.000	3	4	2	0	2	4.50
1921	New York	Amer.	2	9	2	0	1.000	14	10	9	2	9	9.00
1930	New York	Amer.	1	9	1	0	1.000	11	3	3	3	2	3.00
1933	New York	Amer.	1	9	1	0	1.000	12	5	5	0	3	5.00
MAJOR LEAGUE TOTALS			163	1,221	94	46	.671	974	400	309	488	441	2.28

PITCHING / WORLD SERIES

YEAR	CLUB	LEAGUE	G	IP	W	L	PCT.	H	R	ER	SO	BB	ERA
1916	Boston	Amer.	1	14	1	0	1.000	6	1	1	4	3	0.64
1918	Boston	Amer.	2	17	2	0	1.000	13	2	2	4	7	1.06
WORLD SERIES TOTALS			3	31	3	0	1.000	19	3	3	8	10	0.87

KEY

* League leader or tied for league lead.

[1] Ruth is all-time leader in lifetime bases on balls (2,056). Ted Williams is second (2,017).

[2] Home run % (HR%) is number of home runs per 100 times at bat. It is calculated as HR/AB × 100. Lifetime, Ruth homered 8.5% of the time he came to bat; his 8.5% is all-time highest. Ralph Kiner is second (7.1%) and Harmon Killebrew third (7.0%).

[3] AB/HR indicates number of times at bat per home run. Lifetime, Ruth is the all-time leader, with a home run every 11.8 times at bat. Ralph Kiner is second (14.1) and Harmon Killebrew third (14.2).

[4] Slugging average (SA) is total bases divided by times at bat. Ruth's lifetime .690 is all-time highest. Ted Williams is second (.634) and Lou Gehrig third (.632).

INDEX

SOURCES

Innumerable conversations over the past twenty-five years with former teammates and opponents of Babe Ruth, many of whom have since died, have been invaluable in the preparation of this book. For their insights, for their wisdom, and above all for their friendship. We are indebted to Jimmy Austin, Benny Bengough, Rube Bressler, Earle Combs, Stanley Coveleski, Goose Goslin, Hank Greenberg, Heinie Groh, Lefty Grove, Harry Hooper, Waite Hoyt, Sam Jones, Willie Kamm, Lefty O'Doul, Bob O'Farrell, Paul Waner, and Joe Wood, all of whom played with or against the Babe.

We are also grateful to a number of others for helping us with their time and expertise, especially Elaine Chubb, David Falkner, Mark Gallagher, Donald Honig, Phil Kaufman, Bob Kavesh, Fred Lieb, Lee Lowenfish, David Reuther, and John Thorn.

Barry Halper deserves special mention. His generous assistance was invaluable in the preparation of both text and photographs. He gave us access to his unparalleled collection of Babe Ruth memorabilia with patience, enthusiasm and unfailing good humor.

We also wish to extend a special vote of thanks to the following for their outstanding assistance: Michael Aronstein, president of Photo File; Michael Gutierrez, Patricia Kelly of the National Baseball Library; Margaret Miller; Mike Saporito; and Greg Schwalenberg of the Babe Ruth Museum.

For their kind and invaluable assistance in this massive project of image-gathering, we have many, many people to thank: James Bready, Dennis Brearley, Thomas Carwile, Burton F. Clark, Randall Craig, Harriet Culver, Robert Davids, John Dean, Edward "Dutch" Doyle, Greg Drake, Edward W. Earle, Joshua Evans, Ken Felden, Eugene Ferrara, Bill Fitzgerald, Dr. Ron Gabriel, Mark Gallagher, Bruce Garland, Michael Gibbons, Dennis Goldstein, John Grabowski, Tom Heitz, David Horvath, Scott Jahn, Dick Johnson, Lloyd Johnson, David Kemp, Brother Lambert of the Xaverian Brothers, Leonard Levin, Paul Mac Farlane, Ace Marchant, Wayne Martin, Cammie Naylor, Rod Oldfield, C.E. "Pat" Olsen, Ted Patterson, Robert Powers, Joe Sanday, Arthur Schott, John Spalding, Renwick Speer, Harry Staley, Glen Stout, Robert Sui, Jim Sumner, Mark Vartavuk, Rich Wandel, Robert White, Pete Williams, and Charles Winner.

Finally, we would also like to thank our editor, Cork Smith, who has been helpful and supportive from the start, it has been a delight to work with him. And Sylvia Frezzolini's splendid design has done the Babe proud.

There are a number of excellent books about Babe Ruth. His own auto-biography—*The Babe Ruth Story* by Babe Ruth as told to Bob Considine (E. P. Dutton, 1948)—is an indispensible source even though the facts are often a bit askew. Ruth, Considine, and Fred Lieb (who was also involved in the research and writing) worked on the book while Babe was in the throes of his painful terminal illness, so that it was often difficult for Ruth to speak or to concentrate for long.

When Ruth presented the manuscript of the book to Yale University, he said, "You know, you can't put everything in a story, so I left out a few things. Maybe there should have been two books, one for kids and one for adults."

An appropriate companion to Ruth's autobiography is *The Babe and I* by Mrs. Babe Ruth with Bill Slocum (Prentice-Hall, 1959).

There are more than two dozen biographies of Babe Ruth. The five best, listed in alphabetical order by author:

> ROBERT W. CREAMER, *Babe: The Legend Comes to Life* (Simon and Schuster, 1974). Paperback published by Penguin Books in 1983.
>
> MARSHALL SMELSER, *The House That Ruth Built* (Quadrangle, 1975).
>
> KEN SOBOL, *Babe Ruth & The American Dream* (Random House, 1974).
>
> KAL WAGENHEIM, *Babe Ruth: His Life and Legend* (Praeger, 1974).
>
> MARTIN WELDON, *Babe Ruth* (Thomas Y. Crowell, 1948).

Why are Ruth biographies clustered in 1974 and 1975? Because that's when Henry Aaron was breaking Babe Ruth's lifetime home run record. Aaron hit his seven hundred and fourteenth and seven hundred and fifteenth in April 1974. When Aaron broke the Babe's record, hardly any Aaron books appeared, but half a dozen books promptly came out about Babe Ruth.

There are two other books about Ruth that are also worth reading, although they are not as substantial as those mentioned above:

> DAN DANIEL & H. G. SALSINGER, *The Real Babe Ruth* (The Sporting News, 1963).
>
> TOM MEANY, *Babe Ruth: The Big Moments of the Big Fellow* (A. S. Barnes, 1947). Paperback published by Bantam Books in 1948.

Finally, two interesting pamphlets deserve special mention:

> WAITE HOYT, *Babe Ruth as I Knew Him* (Dell, 1948).
>
> LOUIS J. LEISMAN, *I Was with Babe Ruth at St. Mary's* (1956).

PICTURE CREDITS

THE BABE RUTH MUSEUM: p. 15 bot, 20–21, 38 left, 56, 116, 149 bot, 198 top, 209, 215, 221 top, 222 top left & bot, 268 bot, color p. 4 bot right, color p. 5 top, color p. 15 bot.

BETTMANN ARCHIVE: p. 51 top, 79, 143 bot, 246 top.

BETTMANN NEWSPHOTOS: p. 112 top, 130 bot, 202 top, 224 both, 228 bot, 243 bot, 252 bot, 254 top, 261 bot.

BILLY ROSE THEATRE COLLECTION, THE NEW YORK PUBLIC LIBRARY AT LINCOLN CENTER, ASTOR, LENOX, AND TILDEN FOUNDATIONS: p. 190 bot.

BLACK STAR: p. 245.

JAMES H. BREADY: p. 15 top.

COPYRIGHT THE BREARLEY COLLECTION: p. 104 both, 127 bot, 181, 196, 227 top, 229, 251 bot, 260, 261 top, 267.

COURTESY OF THE BRONX COUNTY HISTORICAL SOCIETY COLLECTION, BRONX, NEW YORK: pp. 90–91.

BROWN BROTHERS: p. 57 bot, 114 top, 172, 274.

COURTESY OF THOMAS CARWILE: p. 50 bot, 88 bot right, 89 all, 121 top middle, 163 bot, 220 bot, color p. 6 top left & right & bot right, color p. 10, color p. 11 top, color p. 13, color p. 14 bot left & right.

CLEVELAND PRESS LIBRARY AND COLLECTIONS, CLEVELAND STATE UNIVERSITY LIBRARIES: p. 118 top, 131, 261 middle.

CULVER PICTURES: p. 92, 93, 103, 182 top, 197 bot, 201, 257 bot.

COPYRIGHT JOHN DEAN/BABE RUTH MUSEUM: color p. 1.

KENNETH A. FELDEN: p. 46 both, 52 right, 73 bot.

FREELANCE PHOTOGRAPHERS GUILD: p. 57 top, 70 both, 107, 108, 140 top, 142 bot right, 160 top right, 195, 223 bot, 258 bot, 272 bot.

COURTESY OF DENNIS GOLDSTEIN: p. 87 top, 110 both, 187.

MIKE GUTIERREZ/MARK JORDAN COLLECTION: p. 109 top, 111, 115 top left, 146 top, 148, 157 top, 168 top, 183 bot, 242 top, 243 top.

BARRY HALPER: p. 19 bot, 22, 39, 48–49, 51 bot left, 53, 64, 76–77, 87 bot, 106 right, 118 bot, 120 all, 121 top left & right; bot all, 126 top, 130 top, 139, 143 top, 156 bot, 158 top, 168 bot, 169 top, 173, 174, 182 bot left, 185 bot, 204, 233, 234, 241, 249, 265 bot, color p. 2 all, color p. 4 top & bot left, color p. 5 bot, color p. 7, color p. 12 both, color p. 14 top, color p. 15 top left & right.

HILLERICH & BRADSBY COLLECTION, UNIVERSITY OF LOUISVILLE PHOTOGRAPHIC ARCHIVES: p. 197 top.

INTERNATIONAL MUSEUM OF PHOTOGRAPHY AT GEORGE EASTMAN HOUSE: p. 166, 167 all.

COPYRIGHT KIRK M. KANDLE, ALL RIGHTS RESERVED: p. 206 both.

WILLIAM L. KLENDER: p. 14.

LIBRARY OF CONGRESS: frontice p., 52 left, 75 bot, 106 left, 112 bot, 117 bot, 160 top left.

PAUL MAC FARLANE-MARY BRODERICK: p. 17.

LEROY B. MERRIKEN: p. 182 bot right.

MINNESOTA HISTORICAL SOCIETY: p. 124 top.

NATIONAL ARCHIVES: p. 141 top, 144.

NATIONAL BASEBALL LIBRARY, COOPERSTOWN, N.Y.: p. 6, 18, 23 top, 24, 25 top, 35, 36–37 all, 38 right, 40 bot, 41 top, 43, 45 both, 50 top left & right, 51 bot right, 54–55, 58, 67, 68, 69 both, 71 all, 72 both, 73 top, 74, 75 top, 80, 82 bot, 83, 86 top, 100, 105 both, 109 bot, 114 bot, 115 bot left, 117 top left & right, 119 top, 122, 123 both, 124 bot, 125, 126 bot, 127 top, 128 both, 132, 141 bot, 142 bot left, 146 bot, 147 top, 149 top, 150 bot, 151, 152, 157 bot, 159, 160 bot right, 161 bot, 162 both, 165 both, 169 bot, 170 left, 171, 183 top, 184, 185 top, 186, 188 bot, 190 top left, 191, 192 both, 194 bot, 198 bot, 199 both, 200 both, 202 bot, 203 both, 205 bot, 207, 216 both, 218 both, 219, 223 top, 225 bot, 226 both, 227 bot, 228 top, 231 both, 232, 242 bot, 244 all, 246 bot, 247 both, 248 all, 250 bot, 252 top, 255 both, 256 top, 258 top, 259, 262 bot, 266 both, 270–271, 272 top, 273 both, color p. 9.

NEW YORK DAILY NEWS: p. 3, 82 top, 113, 170 right, 188 top.

COURTESY OF THE NEW-YORK HISTORICAL SOCIETY, NEW YORK: p. 78.

PHOTO FILE: p. VI, 26–27, 44, 81 bot, 86 bot, 115 top right, 119 bot, 129, 140 bot; 142 top, 145, 150–151 top, 153 top, 156 top, 158 bot, 161 top, 163 top, 164, 189, 208, 230, 253 bot, 256 bot, 262 top, 263, 265 top.

PHOTO COURTESY PROVIDENCE JOURNAL-BULLETIN: p. 40 top.

LAWRENCE RITTER: p. 81 top, 94, 190 top right, 193 both, 217, 222 top right, 254 bot.

MARK RUCKER: p. 250 top, color p. 6 bot left, color p. 8 top left & right.

FROM THE LIBRARY OF ARTHUR O. SCHOTT, BASEBALL HISTORIAN: p. 251 top.

JOHN SPALDING-PHOTOGRAPHY BY BARRY COLLA: color p. 11 bot.

THE SPORTING NEWS: p. 28, 88 top, 147 bot, 225 top.

JOHN THORN: p. 84, 85, 153 bot, 154–155, color pg. 8 bot.

THE WESTERN RESERVE HISTORICAL SOCIETY, CLEVELAND, OHIO: p. 47.

ROBERT L. WHITE: color p. 3.

WIDE WORLD: p. 194 top, 220 top, 221 bot, 253 top, 257 top, 264, 269.

CHARLES S. WINNER: p. 19 top, 23 bot.

ROBERT K. WOOD: p. 41 bot, 42, 268 top.

XAVERIAN BROTHERS, KENSINGTON, MD.: p. 10, 16 both, 25 bot.

VANITY FAIR: color p. 16.